Good Clean Violence

Good Clean Violence

A HISTORY OF COLLEGE FOOTBALL

Ivan N. Kaye

J.B. LIPPINCOTT COMPANY
Philadelphia and New York

U.S. Library of Congress Cataloging in Publication Data

Kaye, Ivan N
    Good clean violence.

    Bibliography: p.
    1. Football—History. I. Title.
    GV950.K39   796.33′263′09   73–781
    ISBN–0–397–00964–X

ACKNOWLEDGMENTS

Barrie Van Dyck of Lippincott edited this book. Don Bender of Lippincott designed it. John Looney of United Press International found the illustrations for it. And Edward L. Burlingame, Editor-in-Chief of Lippincott, believed in it.

All photographs not otherwise attributed are courtesy of United Press International.

Contents

List of Illustrations

8

H.K.
B.D.K.

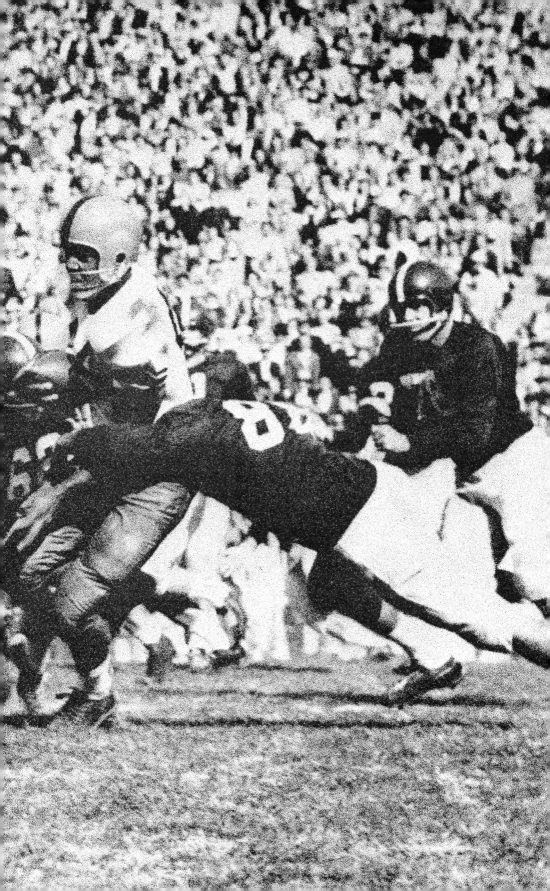

"What's wrong with a little good clean violence?"

> —Robert Timberlake, Michigan '65, All-America quarterback, in reply to a questioner who had asked how he, a preministerial student, could justify taking part in football.

Good Clean Violence

1. In the Beginning

The origins of football, a game which embraces the elements of chess, geometry, and warfare, remain lost somewhere in the immemorial past.

It is known that the ancient Greeks played a game they called "harpaston" involving a small round ball which was batted with the hand, and that the action took place on a ruled field. But, strangely, neither harpaston nor anything similar to it found its way into the Olympics. Since the Olympic Games included all the sports popular at the time, the omission of any mention of a ball game has caused scholars to doubt that harpaston enjoyed any wide acceptance among the citizens of Hellas.

There are also unverified speculations that the ancient Chinese played some kind of game with a ball. In his book *Athletics of the Ancient World*, Dr. E. Norman Gardiner quotes the nineteenth-century Professor H. A. Giles: "An old Chinese writer, speaking of the town of Lin-tzu, says there were none among its inhabitants who did not perform with pipes or some string instrument, fight cocks, race dogs, or play football."

Professor Giles also wrote that a round ball made of eight pointed strips of leather and filled with air was used in China around A.D. 500. Giles's findings, however, have been denigrated by *Menke's Encyclopedia of Sports* and are under suspicion generally by football historians.

There are also largely unsubstantiated speculations that the Roman emperor Augustus Caesar (63 B.C. – A.D. 14) banned a game similar to harpaston (which the Romans called "harpastum") as being too gentle to fit soldiers for war. There is no documentation for this Augustinian edict, but since the Romans did appropriate numerous Greek cultural institutions when they conquered the city-states, it is reasonable to assume that they copied Greek athletics as well.

The Romans may have brought some kind of ball game to Britain when they invaded it two thousand years ago. It is also possible that the islanders initiated a kick-ball form of amusement on their own. In any event, by the eleventh century a game resembling a rudimentary form of soccer was in evidence in England. One possible origination may have occurred around the year 1050, when some English workmen unearthed the skull of one of their former Danish overlords. It is certain that the discoverer did not pick up the skull and say something like "alas poor Yorick," since it was still half a millennium before the Bard. But it is quite believable that, having little affection for the remains of one of his former conquerors, he gave the skull a vicious kick and sent it bounding along the ground. The digger's colleagues are thought to have returned the gesture, and some observing boys, it is speculated, took up the diversion when the men went back to work. Since the youngsters were barefoot, legend has it that they quickly stubbed their toes at "kicking the Dane's head," as the amusement became known. One of their number, perhaps the real father of football, sought something softer and came up with an inflated cow's bladder.

Soon groups of boys and young men were kicking these primitive footballs back and forth from village to village. There was little or no form to the game, no rules, and no specified number of participants. There was a good deal of free-lance rowdyism attending the proceedings, and it is believed that the more prudent residents locked up their silver and their womenfolk when they saw the kicking and screaming horde approaching. The confining of the game to a specified field may have come about through the efforts of village elders who wanted to ensure the safety of their streets.

A game called play ball was evident in London by the year 1175. It was held annually on Shrove Tuesday both in the capital and in the walled city of Chester. Eventually both King Henry VIII and Queen Elizabeth I prohibited the game, saying that it was distracting the soldiers from archery, which the monarchs thought a much more useful sport for the military. This attitude contrasts strongly with the view of modern generals such as Douglas MacArthur, who, when he was in charge at West Point, said that the two games he wanted the cadets to learn were football and chess.

The soccerlike kicking game continued to be played in England without significant change in form, except for the standardizing of the field and the number of players, until one cold November afternoon in 1823.

It was nearing five o'clock on the playing fields of Rugby School, and the bell would soon toll the finish of the day's soccer match. William Webb Ellis, frustrated at the prospect of an impending tie, suddenly scooped up the ball and ran with it over his opponents' goal. In the consternation which followed, Ellis was called a spoilsport, a rotter, and a bloody subversive. Everyone agreed that what he had done was not soccer, and most added that it was not cricket either. Indeed it was neither. It was Rugby, the forerunner of the American game of football.

Oddly enough, however, when football did make its appearance at New Brunswick some forty-six years later in the epic game between Princeton and Rutgers, it was essentially soccer and not Rugby that the two teams played.

In England during the decades after Ellis' celebrated improvisation the game of football proceeded along two divergent paths. Some played soccer, while others, perhaps hardier or more attuned to mayhem, played Rugby. But still it took more than twenty years before the idea of running with the ball was formally accepted and the game of Rugby achieved something like equal status with soccer.

In early America there had been various forms of kicking games played at colleges and secondary schools. Harvard had a festival in the early 1800s which qualified vaguely as football. It was called Bloody Monday, but the upperclassmen mostly kicked the freshmen and only occasionally the ball.

At Princeton and nearby Rutgers the intramural rivalries

were overshadowed by a long-continuing struggle for possession of an abandoned Revolutionary War cannon. A raiding party would set out from the school which lacked the cannon, and with grim and faultless execution purloin the rusty fieldpiece and pull it, bouncing, over the dusty roads back to its campus.

This went on for years until a reactionary bunch of Princetonians stole the gun from New Brunswick and planted it in concrete. The men of Rutgers were outraged, and to assuage their fury Princeton accepted a challenge to play baseball. Princeton won the game by a score of 40–2, and the Rutgers men began casting about for another sport.

Football seemed the perfect answer. On the afternoon of November 6, 1869, at New Brunswick, twenty-five students from Princeton met a like number from Rutgers in the first intercollegiate football game. The rules differed from soccer only in that players could run ahead of the kicker as a sort of interference, which resembled a primitive form of blocking. They could also catch or bat the ball with their hands. Running with the ball was strictly prohibited, however, and nobody had even dreamed that it might be thrown through the air.

Some fifty fans accompanied the Princeton team. The hosts took their guests to a meal and then on a short tour of the campus, after which all adjourned to the athletic field for the game. The players performed in shirt sleeves, with the Rutgers men wearing scarlet bandannas around their heads.

Princeton had the taller and stronger players, but Rutgers enjoyed greater speed and mobility, and kicked the six goals which signified victory, while holding the visitors to four.

One Rutgers man became confused and kicked the ball toward his own goal, enabling Princeton to score. Thus in the first football game there was the precursor of Roy Riegels' celebrated wrong-way run sixty years hence in the Rose Bowl.

After the game there was another meal, the Princetonians were put aboard the evening train, and promises were exchanged that there would be another game on the following Saturday. The happy Rutgers men then withdrew to savor their triumph with wine and song (but probably no women, since they were, after all, in training), and it is remembered that the sound of their jubilant choruses rose in the night along the banks of the Old Raritan. It was good that they so enjoyed their victory, for in one of the most remarkable jinxes of the sport, it would be sixty-nine years and thirty-five contests before Rutgers would beat Princeton again in a game of football.

2. Harvard Holds Out

Princeton won the return match a week later on its home grounds. It was in this game that organized cheering first made its appearance. A week earlier some of the Princeton players had sought to unnerve the Rutgers men by giving out with rebel yells when Rutgers had the ball. This psychological warfare backfired, however, since the Rutgers men retained their composure and the Princetonians found to their dismay that they could not run and yell at the same time without becoming winded. During the next week, the Princeton players succeeded in training a number of their classmates in coordinated shouting, and, although the noise had no bearing upon the outcome, it became an established part of the proceedings thereafter.

A third match was agreed upon, but the faculties of both schools, fearing an overemphasis, objected, and the affair was canceled. But the game was already spreading, and after a few years Columbia, Yale, and Stevens Tech took it up. The game these schools were playing was soccer, but when Harvard moved into the picture, it pressed for a version which had been played in the Boston area by secondary schools and which allowed a player to run with the ball until he was pursued.

In the autumn of 1873 Harvard refused to join with Princeton, Rutgers, Columbia, and Yale in codifying rules for a soccerlike game. Harvard held out for the Boston game, as its version was called, and by its refusal to join the other schools made perhaps the most momentous decision in the history of

American football. If Harvard had gone along, the five universities would then have set up rules for soccer, and in all probability that—and not football as it is now played—would have become the major collegiate sport.

Since Harvard, befitting the alma mater of Henry David Thoreau, had elected to march to the sound of a different drummer, it had to look elsewhere for an opponent. In the spring of the following year it invited McGill University of Montreal to come down to Cambridge for a two-game competition.

The first match, on May 14, 1874, was conducted under Harvard's Boston-game rules, and the hosts won easily. The next day the two schools played to a tie under McGill's Canadian Rugby rules, which allowed a player to pick up the ball and run with it whether or not he was pursued. The fans and the Harvard men immediately took to the McGill style, and thus it was the celebrated Canadian university which played a seminal role in the establishment of the American game of football.

Harvard converted its ancient rival Yale the following year by defeating it four goals to none. This was the first of what not only the adherents of both schools but also most of the football world as well would soon come to call The Game.

Even though they lost, the Yale players and fans liked the running game and quickly forgot about soccer. Although running was now the dominant method of advancing the ball, the kick was still the only way to score. To run the ball over the opponent's goal line brought no points as it does today. The touchdown meant only that the privilege of a free kick had been obtained. A successful kick meant a score of one goal. In succeeding years all this would change, with the touchdown gradually achieving parity with the kicked goal and finally surpassing both it and the field goal. Eventually even the extra-point rule would be modified when, in 1958, it became possible to try for two points by either running or passing.

Football made its first appearance outside the East in the last year of the seventies. The University of Michigan inaugurated the game in the Midwest, meeting Racine College at the old White Stockings Baseball Park in Chicago on May 30, 1879. The team from Ann Arbor won the game and scheduled another with the same opponent in the autumn, as well as one with the University of Toronto.

In 1881 Michigan journeyed East to play the first intersectional game. It lost to Harvard by one goal to nothing. Yale and Princeton, each playing its first intersectional opponent, also defeated Michigan. The Midwesterners returned to Ann Arbor, wrote off their Eastern tour as an educational experience, and abandoned football the following year.

But in 1883 Michigan came East for another try at the Establishment. It bowed in a close game to Harvard, was annihilated by Yale, lost respectably to Wesleyan, and earned a gratifying five-goal-to-one victory over Stevens Tech. A game with Cornell, to be played at the neutral site of Cleveland, was proposed, but that school's president, Andrew White, who had once taught history at Ann Arbor, vetoed it with the classic statement: "I shall not permit thirty men to travel four hundred miles merely to agitate a bag of wind."

Four years later another wandering Michigan team was received with great hospitality in South Bend, Indiana, where it taught the fundamentals of the game to the local men's college, Notre Dame.

Paradoxically, just as football was beginning to spread to other sections of the country, some apparently insoluble problems began to develop in the game itself. It was essentially a Rugbylike style of play that was in evidence in the early eighties. The ball was kicked or run with in a free-form manner with no attempt at strategic planning.

Walter Camp, a player and later the coach at Yale, yearned to impose some order and coherence upon the game. To effect this, Camp, who is generally considered the father of football as we know it, proposed the idea of the scrimmage. Instead of dropping the ball between the contending teams, as had been done in Rugby (and still is in soccer), Camp would give possession to one side and allow it to plan offensive movements. The side lacking possession of the ball would have to content itself with stopping its opponent. When a score was made, the teams would exchange control of the ball.

Walter Camp of Yale, the "father of American football." The sight of blood caused him to grow faint.

This sounded fine and seemed to give the game a considerable stylistic boost—to create a kind of violent chess, as it were. But when Yale and Princeton played their notorious "block game" in 1881, it became obvious that the invention of the scrimmage represented merely a lifting of the lid of Pandora's box.

Yale discovered that it could retain possession of the ball for an entire half, and Princeton found, likewise, that it could hold it for the whole of the second half. Each team was content with the prospect of a stalemate because each felt that it could claim the championship if it remained undefeated. Such conservatism roused the ire of the fans and many of the players as well, and nearly all agreed that something had to be done.

To this challenge, in true Toynbeean fashion, there arose a most far-reaching response. Again it came from the inventive brain of Walter Camp, who was to forsake a medical career because he grew faint in the presence of blood. He proposed a system of "downs," or tries, under which a team had to advance the ball 5 yards (or be thrown for a loss of 10 yards) in order to retain possession. The 10-yard-loss provision faded out later, and the essentials of the modern game were fixed. Eventually the yardage-to-be-gained requirement was set at 10 in four downs.

With the ground rules having achieved a measure of stability, attention turned to the more mundane business of winning games. Through the later eighties and on up to the beginning of the new century, Yale, Princeton, Harvard, and Pennsylvania dominated football. Yale, in particular, not only established hegemony on the field but also sent its best players into the hinterlands to found dynasties which soon began to rival that of their alma mater. Amos Alonzo Stagg, an end on Walter Camp's first All-America, became the first coach at the new University of Chicago in 1892. He was destined to remain for forty-one years on the Midway, turning out a number of excellent teams and hundreds of first-rate players, including most notably Walter Eckersall, the best quarterback of the pre-forward-pass era. Also from New Haven went Dr. Henry L. Williams to take up the coaching chair at the University of Minnesota in 1900. Dr. Williams, who also lectured in gynecology at the Minnesota medical school, had earned his M.D. at the University of Pennsylvania. He turned out twenty-two Minnesota teams, nearly all of them formidable and several downright awesome. In general, the star players of the big four Eastern teams who entered coaching either stayed at their own school or left for the provinces. Seldom did a Harvard star coach at Princeton or Yale, or vice versa. One prominent exception, however, was George Woodruff, an all-time great guard at Yale. He took the helm at the University of Pennsylvania in 1891 and guided that school to the most successful decade in its long football history. Princeton men were active too in spreading the style and methods of the Eastern Establishment, notably Phil King, who lifted Wisconsin's early teams to sectional eminence, and Knowleton "Snake" Ames, a pioneer in Purdue's embryonic football program.

Yale, as Grantland Rice would write in his poem years later, was still "King of the conquered East." But Princeton most often presented the sternest challenge, and when the two collided in 1888, the mythical championship was once again the prize. The Tigers came prepared with a new stratagem, which had enabled them to terrorize Pennsylvania. It was called the V trick, and it presented a moving triangle of interlocked players, with the point of the V directed at the opponent's goal and the ballcarrier ensconced in the middle. Consternation swept the Yale ranks until this seemingly insoluble dilemma was resolved in a brilliant and daring defensive maneuver by Yale's greatest player, William Walter "Pudge" Heffelfinger. The almost legendary Heffelfinger, who many believe was the best guard of all time, ran at full speed toward the apex of the triangle, leaped high enough so that he vaulted over the leading blockers, and landed his two hundred pounds knees-first on the astounded ballcarrier. This gesture, almost suicidal for anyone with less heft and coordination, succeeded in throttling Princeton, and the Bulldogs won the game. But few elevens had a Heffelfinger to smash an enemy's V trick. Many teams began to base their offense on the play. The game thus became rougher than ever and took

William Walter "Pudge" Heffelfinger of Yale. Shades of Frank Merri-well.

on more and more of the aspects of a massed street brawl. Indeed, line play was little better than that anyway, with no neutral zone between the contending forwards. Often they simply stood toe-to-toe, or perhaps eyeball-to-eyeball, not merely until someone blinked but until he got a black eye as well.

For all its destructiveness, however, the V trick was a rather slow-moving alignment. It remained for Harvard to add the element of momentum to create the truly devastating and even lethal "flying wedge," the most talked-about play of the nineties. The maneuver was invented, oddly enough, not by a player or a coach but by a devoted Harvard fan and chess master, Loren F. DeLand, who had never even played foot-ball. On kickoffs and other open-field plays, two lines would

26

converge at high speed with the ballcarrier in the middle. By the time the wedge had gathered momentum, getting in its way was roughly akin to facing down a freight train under full steam. As usual in football, the defenses attempted to cope with the flying wedge, but they were successful only when they could offer stupefyingly brutal force in return. Thus when a team with any kind of weight advantage used the flying wedge, it had a virtually invincible weapon on offense.

The wedge was but one of a number of new formations which stressed the principle of massed players moving at great momentum toward a given point. Alonzo Stagg stationed ends in the backfield; George Woodruff, who had performed so brilliantly as a running guard at Yale, placed his guards in the backfield while coaching at Pennsylvania. The "guards back" formation enabled the Quakers to concentrate awesome blocking ahead of their ballcarriers and was the principal reason for Penn's 124 victories and only 15 losses during Woodruff's decade.

All of these strategic developments were predicated on force rather than on speed or deception. Momentum times mass made for a mathematical formula which more often than not assured victory for the team which could muster the bigger numbers.

The new techniques of offense forced smaller and faster men out of the game and put a premium on sheer tonnage. There was also an alarming rise in fatalities and serious injuries. Nearly all players disdained headgear (they grew enormous shocks of hair to cushion the impact of collisions), and there was nothing like the padding or the taping of vulnerable joints that would come along later with the arrival of professional trainers.

A movement arose to ban the more destructive of the mass-momentum formations. This resulted in bitterness among the big four of the Eastern Establishment, with Harvard and Pennsylvania favoring retention of the guards-back formation, with which they had been enjoying great success, and Yale and Princeton calling for its abolition.

A compromise of sorts was reached in 1896 when limitations were imposed on the use of the mass-momentum plays and the flying wedge was outlawed on kickoffs. Although it would be another decade before the massed formations would be legislated out of existence, the trend clearly began moving back toward speed and deception as the new century dawned.

Appropriately, the coach who personified this concern with rapidity bore the sobriquet Hurry-Up. He was Fielding Harris Yost, a former tackle at Lafayette, deputy sheriff in some of West Virginia's gamier mining towns, barrister, and wandering football tutor at Ohio Wesleyan, Nebraska, Kansas, Stanford, and, finally, the University of Michigan.

3.The Game Catches On

Even in the nineties the Midwest was on the way toward establishing a big four of its own (Chicago, Michigan, Wisconsin, and Minnesota) to rival the Eastern giants. Michigan, well before the arrival of Yost in 1901, was turning out strong elevens. One of them went East in 1895 and held Harvard to a field goal, a respectable showing despite the fact that Michigan failed to score. Wisconsin, too, fielded strong teams and also challenged an Eastern power, Yale. The Badgers lost by a touchdown, but their performance underscored the point that there were formidable teams rising in the heartland, albeit perhaps not quite yet of the caliber of the old titans of the Atlantic seaboard.

In the eighteen seasons from 1883 to 1900 Yale lost only 9 games (6 to Princeton, 2 to Harvard, and 1 to Columbia), while winning 197. Three of her teams held all opponents scoreless (1888, 1891, and 1892, while registering 694, 488, and 435 points respectively themselves), one gave up only a field goal (1886), and another only a safety (1883). Seven perfect seasons and four marred only by ties were achieved. For sustained excellence over an entire generation, the Old Blue stood unmatched, but its perennial challenger, Princeton, compiled an enviable record of its own.

The Tigers lost only 16 times (10 to Yale, 2 each to Pennsylvania and Cornell, and 1 each to Harvard and Columbia), while winning 175. There were three perfect seasons and four others with one tie game.

In the 18 meetings during those years between the two

29

superpowers, the record stood at 10 victories for Yale, 6 for Princeton, and 2 deadlocks. On six occasions Yale handed Princeton its only defeat of the year; four times the Tigers returned the compliment, and both tie games saw the teams enter with perfect records. Nearly always the meeting between the Bulldogs and the Tigers was the final game of the year for both, and, at least in this era, Princeton, and not Harvard, was Yale's great rival.

If Harvard and Pennsylvania could not quite match the glitter of the teams with animal nicknames, the Cantabridgians and the Quakers nonetheless turned out consistently strong, and occasionally titanic, teams.

Pennsylvania, in particular, prospered in the mid-nineties under George Woodruff, fielding three perfect-record squads (1894, 1895, and 1897), and winning 65 out of 66 encounters during the period. Only the heralded Lafayette team of 1896, itself undefeated, succeeded in lowering Pennsylvania's proud red-and-blue banners, and then only by a 6–4 score.

Harvard sent out all-victorious teams in 1890 and again in 1898. The Crimson's all-time star lineman, Marshall "Ma" Newell, a watch-charm tackle at 167 pounds, was the hero of the 1890 season. Harvard would yet enjoy its vintage years, however, with the promotion of another of its linemen, the brilliant, moody, and enigmatic Percy D. Haughton, to the coaching chair in 1908.

Because of disputes over rough play in previous games, or eligibility standards, there were many seasons in which one or more of the Big Four did not play the others. This led to interminable wrangling over which was the Eastern champion —which meant national champion as well, since in those days it was taken for granted that the best in the East was the best anywhere. The problem remains to this day, only on a national scale, with nearly all students of the game expressing disenchantment with the results of the wire-service polls.

Also, the big-name schools were guilty of inflating their winning percentages at the expense of badly undermanned opponents. Yale wrought carnage upon Wesleyan not once but often two or three times in some seasons, and Princeton

30

likewise pillaged Stevens Tech without pity. The practice was shared, at least in the early years, by all of the big-name teams, including Notre Dame, Michigan, Minnesota, Alabama, Tennessee, Georgia Tech, Texas, Oklahoma, and others.

It was to establish both a relative parity in schedules and a general agreement on eligibility standards that the idea of a conference, or league, of football playing universities was born. At the behest of President Smart of Purdue, his school and the Big Four of the Midwest, joined by Northwestern and Illinois, founded the Western Conference in 1895. Iowa and Indiana were admitted shortly after, and Ohio State entered in 1912. Chicago withdrew after World War II and was replaced by Michigan State.

Thus was the Big Ten born. In the years that followed, especially after the First World War, it would come to dominate college football, and its champion, year in and year out, would be considered either the nation's best team or surely among the top two or three. In recent times, however, the conference has suffered a serious decline, perhaps best exemplified by the fact that its champions have lost six of the last eight Rose Bowl games.

Wisconsin won the first two Big Ten titles and stayed near the top for most of the league's first decade, as did Chicago, Minnesota, and Michigan. This was no surprise, since these were the sectional leaders even before the conference was founded.

Wisconsin had its greatest football hero ever during these years. He was Pat O'Dea, an Australian with a kick like that of a kangaroo. He may well have been the finest kicker the game of football has ever produced. Field goals of 50 and 60 yards were the rule with O'Dea rather than the exception. He was more of an offensive threat with a dropkick than nearly anyone else was when running with the ball. In that era the rounded-end football made drop-kicking relatively easy, and the offenses of successful teams were sometimes constructed around the field goal rather than the touchdown. It was difficult to run through massed defenses, and touchdowns were purchased dearly, but if a team had a really good dropkicker it could score from anywhere closer than midfield. Thus the Wisconsin teams prospered, and O'Dea should have been everyone's All-America choice.

The fact that he missed universal acclaim derived largely from a certain provincialism on the part of Walter Camp and Casper Whitney, the two experts who chose the All-America teams. Camp's selections, in particular, carried the greatest prestige. It may have been asking too much of this unquestioned genius of the early football years to have realized the vastly improved caliber of players in the Midwest. It was true, after all, that for the first quarter of a century the really good performers had been found on the Eastern fields. And who could have blamed Camp if he demurred at leaving New Haven or Princeton on game day to travel into the provinces and observe some clumsy yokel in Iowa just because the hometown press was insisting that it had an overlooked All-America there?

So for many years players in the Midwest, South, Southwest, and West labored in obscure vineyards when it came to All-America recognition. They did not seem to perform less well for all that, however. And in later years, when Camp did journey to places like Chicago and Minneapolis and Ann Arbor, he was pleased to make some amends and place stars like Eckersall of Chicago, Heston of Michigan, and McGovern of Minnesota on his first teams.

Probably nothing except the argument over which school deserves the national championship has aroused football partisans as much over the years as the All-America selections. Today there are so many different appraisers that a player at almost any big-name school who shows talent will win some kind of recognition. But in the old days it was a matter of impressing Camp or Whitney. If a player did very well in a particular game which was witnessed by either of the selectors, he might be placed on the All-America first team on the basis of one afternoon's inspired play. The spirited performance of Michigan's Johnny Maulbetsch, albeit in a losing cause, against Harvard at Cambridge in 1915 and Gaylord Stinchcomb's heroics for Ohio State in winning the Wisconsin game in 1920 were two examples of Camp's bestowing All-

America kudos for one standout effort. There is still no way to recognize properly the gifts of a player on a small-college team, although professional football has gone a long way toward focusing attention upon the high caliber of athletes coming from the lesser-known schools. It is interesting to note that the two colleges which had the largest number of seniors drafted by the professionals after the 1969 season were Southern California and Grambling.

If the Midwestern players were not yet receiving their due, there could be no doubt in anyone's mind where the best of the coaches lived. Amos Alonzo Stagg, the Yale end on Walter Camp's first All-America, had forsaken an even more promising career as a baseball player and come west to the brand new University of Chicago to become its first, and for the next forty-one years its only, coach of football. The university had sprung almost from the brow (or perhaps, more accurately, from the checkbook) of the Cleveland Croesus, John D. Rockefeller. It was, its detractors said, a kind of instant Harvard, without any of the traditions of that oldest and most revered of American universities. But when Chicago began luring scholars from the established schools, and especially when it tempted John Dewey away from Michigan, everyone knew that it had become a force to be reckoned with. On the gridiron too the maroon banners of Stagg's first teams waved much more often in victory than such upstarts had a right to expect. In Ann Arbor, in particular, where the old, proud University of Michigan had long reveled in the glory of being known as the "Harvard of the West," it was galling in the extreme not only to lose faculty lights to the latecomer on the Midway but to bow on the gridiron to it as well. Chicago's Thanksgiving Day game with Michigan became the Midwestern equivalent of Harvard versus Yale. And especially in the years just after the turn of the century, when Hurry-Up Yost came upon the scene, it witnessed some of the best football and football players of all time.

To play for Alonzo Stagg was to play for the most inventive coach of the era, perhaps of any era. What Stagg did not invent, young Glenn Scobey Warner, recently departed from Cornell to make the Carlisle Indians the scourge of the East,

Amos Alonzo Stagg, the Grand Old Man of football, celebrating his ninety-third birthday in 1955. He was to live for another nine years.

would. Stagg was pioneering in maneuvers such as the lateral, the reverse, the man-in-motion, unbalanced lines, cross-blocking, backfield shifts, and unorthodox defenses. And even then Warner was tinkering with the idea of stationing a halfback a step outside of the end to ensure a perfect blocking angle on the opposing tackle and also to set up the deep reverse. Warner's single wingback formation, as he called it, was to sweep the coaching profession in a few years and remain for a generation the favorite offense of most of the powers, until he himself came along with something even more inventive.

Stagg's teams, in common with many others in the pre-single-wing era, ran from the T formation, with the quarterback lateraling the ball to a running back after taking it from the center. The T formation was thus the basic attack plan of the old-time game, but it only superficially resembled the modern T formation which so altered the style of play after 1940. The old T formation maneuvers were based on powerful thrusts over guard and tackle and speedy dashes around the ends, and since there was no forward passing threat, the defenses bunched at the scrimmage line to check it.

When defenses begin responding, as they always do, to a hitherto successful offensive tactic, it usually happens that some inventive coach comes up with a new stratagem. Stagg's fellow Yale man, Dr. Henry L. Williams, who had taken over at Minnesota in 1900, popularized the devastating "Minnesota shift," in which his players jumped into a new position at the instant the ball was put into play, thus outflanking the defense, which usually was caught flat-footed. The shift gave its perpetrators both momentum and blocking angles, perhaps the two crucial elements in a successful running game. Controversy over shifts was to flare up many times in later years, reaching almost a frenzy during the 1920s, when dazed victims of Knute Rockne's Notre Dame teams sought relief in rules changes. The legislation which eventually reduced the shift's effectiveness called for a complete, full-second stop before the ball was snapped. This took away the momentum advantage, which in Dr. Williams' era made the huge Minnesota players dreaded opponents.

The new strategies and styles of play were being carried to

the far corners of the land as the old century expired. The East was still the fount, with Yale sending its former star quarterback Mike Donohue to build the teams at Auburn, and John W. Heisman moving into Atlanta to make Georgia Tech an early Southern leader. In a few years Dan McGugin, one of Yost's best and smartest Michigan players, would establish Vanderbilt as the South's strongest team. Tennessee and Alabama were beginning to catch on to the new game, but the years when they were to dominate Dixie football were still far off.

The game was also spreading to the West Coast, where Stagg helped to popularize it by bringing Chicago to play Stanford in 1894. The Palo Alto school—like Chicago, a brand new university—had already inaugurated its series with the arch rival University of California at Berkeley. The meetings would eventually acquire the status of the "Big Game" on the Coast, but when the rivalry began in 1892, it almost did not start at all. The harassed manager of California had to confess to his Stanford counterpart that he had forgotten to bring the football. So, too, had the Stanford manager, whose name was Herbert Clark Hoover.

Such goings-on gave the game a charming, amateurish quality on the Coast. But back in the Midwest, where they always remembered to bring the ball, the teams that went into Ann Arbor after the turn of the century to face Hurry-Up Yost and his mercurial Michigan sometimes wished they had not.

4. A Point a Minute

When Charlie Baird walked down the hill to the Ann
Arbor railroad depot on that cool spring morning in 1901
to meet the new football coach he had hired, he could not
possibly have foreseen that an era was beginning. Baird was
Michigan's graduate manager of athletics, and the tall young
man—just turned thirty—with the shaggy hair and the high,
starched collar who stepped down from the train was Fielding
Harris Yost.

As the two walked back up the hill toward the campus,
Baird inquired how Yost was going to go about rebuilding
Michigan's depressed football team, which had sustained several defeats the previous year, including another galling loss
to Stagg and Chicago.

"Mr. Baird," said Yost in his West Virginia drawl, "there
are three things that make a winner: spirit, manpower, and
coaching. If your boys love Meechigan [he could never say
it right], that takes care of the spirit. If they'll turn out, that
takes care of the manpower. I'll take care of the coaching."

He did not mention anything about recruiting. But this
was by no means an omission peculiar to Yost. Practically
no coach, or even historian of the game, has seen fit to dwell
upon such a grubby reality. It is simply easier to believe that
the large and swift academicians who have graced a thousand
varsities were all deposited as foundlings on the coach's
doorstep.

Recruiting, or ivory hunting, as it has sometimes been

called, probably goes back to the first time one team lost and decided not to lose again. The most that the deans and registrars could hope for was that the coach would seek only intelligent athletes capable of doing college work. That this has sometimes been too Panglossian an expectation has made for fewer Phi Beta Kappas and more All-Americas.

In recent years large alumni booster organizations have arisen at nearly every big-time football school. These talent scouts toil so zealously on behalf of coach and campus that now and then the rules of proselyting are bent—sometimes beyond all recognition. But such things, so we are told, are part of the game, along with clipping, piling on, and roughing the passer.

The varsity which Yost confronted on the first day of practice that fall bore no evidence of a zealous recruiting program, or of any program at all, for that matter. Such efforts were only embryonic then. It was not that the players were untalented—far from it. There were a number of quite good ones, but they had experienced two disappointing seasons, mainly because of uninspired coaching and a certain absence of spark in their offensive maneuvers.

There was, however, one new face among them. Yost, while coaching at Stanford in 1900, had also drilled the San Jose Teachers College team in his spare time. On that little-known squad he had observed one incredibly gifted athlete who, even then, Yost realized was the greatest football player he would ever see. He was William Martin Heston of Grant's Pass, Oregon. Just a shade under 6 feet in height, weighing 190 pounds, faster in a 40-yard sprint than perhaps anyone alive, this young man was hell-bent on doing two things: playing football and studying law. The two men became fast friends, and when Yost accepted the Michigan offer, he asked Heston to come along. Willie Heston had heard little about the Michigan football team, but he was well aware that Michigan had a superb law school. (There are those in Palo Alto who insist to this day that Yost offered financial rewards to Heston and another player, Dad Gregory, who also appeared headed for the Stanford varsity.)

Yost put all the ingredients together in his first season

William Martin Heston of Grant's Pass, Oregon, and the University of Michigan. A funny thing happened on the way to Palo Alto.

Copyrighted 1903, By
Rentschler, Ann Arbor

Heston

and not only launched the most astounding succession of winning teams the game had yet seen, but also presented the first successful challenge to the Eastern dominance of the gridiron.

From the opening kickoff of the 1901 season until practically the last moment of 1905 the Michigan Juggernaut, as it came to be called, rolled through fifty-six games without defeat, winning fifty-five, tying one, and scoring 2,821 points to 40 for all opponents. It still stands as the greatest undefeated streak in the annals of college football. (The University of Washington's sixty-three-game undefeated record, extending from 1908 through 1916, includes nine games with high schools. Thus Michigan holds the mark for intercollegiate play.)

Michigan outscored its opposition by such an incredible margin that writers, exhausting all of their superlatives, fell back upon statistics and labeled the five squads collectively as the "point-a-minute" teams. They did not quite match that figure, but they came remarkably close. In 1901 it was 550 points to 0 in eleven victories. In 1902 it was 644 to 12, also in eleven victories. In 1903 it was 565 to 6 in eleven wins and one tie with Minnesota, one of the classic football encounters. In 1904 the score was 567 to 22 in ten triumphs. In 1905 the first twelve games were won with a total of 495 points to 0 for the opposition.

The caliber of the adversaries, of course, varied. There were a number of small schools on the schedule, but there were also the leading teams of the Midwest, such as Wisconsin, Minnesota, Notre Dame, Northwestern, and most important of all, Stagg's Chicago. The scores achieved in some of the victories are almost unbelievable: 130–0 over West Virginia, Buffalo beaten 128–0, Michigan State 119–0, Iowa 107–0, Ohio State 86–0, Indiana 60–0.

There is no way of knowing how the point-a-minute teams would have fared against the East's best. Whether they could have beaten Harvard's great club of 1901, Yale's of 1902, the Princeton team of 1903, or Pennsylvania's 1904 powerhouse was the most furiously disputed football argument of the day. Where one lived usually determined which side of the argu-

40

ment one took. As far as size and spirit, Michigan was easily comparable to the best the East had. The one attribute which might have tipped the scales in favor of the Wolverine teams was their extraordinary overall speed, not only in carrying out their blocking and running maneuvers but also in calling and setting in motion the plays themselves. This was all part of Yost's system. There was no huddle then, and his quarterbacks, the brilliant Harrison "Boss" Weeks in 1901–02 and Fred Norcross in 1903–04, were instructed to call the signals for the next play while the teams were picking themselves up from the ground after the last one. The effect was devastating, with opponents having practically no opportunity to set up defenses or to regroup themselves psychologically, and Yost fully appreciated the emotional impact of a successful touchdown march.

He also devoted enormous energy to defense, and here the efforts of the point-a-minute clubs were no less spectacular than their offensive performance. To give up only six touchdowns in five years is all but unbelievable. The 1901 team was so strong defensively that the longest gain made by an opponent was 15 yards, the deepest enemy advance was to the Michigan 30-yard line, and none of the ten regular-season foes, nor Stanford in the first Rose Bowl game, came close to scoring. In later years, when Yost lacked the great offensive stars who had so distinguished these teams, his defensive philosophy dominated not only his own squads but, because of his prestige, the thinking of other coaches as well. Yost came to believe that games were generally lost through some opponent's blunder rather than won by offensive strategy. Thus he built his defense first, anchoring it with a strong, mobile center who backed up the line. It was no accident that in Adolph "Germany" Schulz he developed probably the finest operative at this position that the game ever produced. The sturdy defensive line was abetted by a good punter who would continually keep the ball deep in the opponent's territory. The idea was to play for field position, a fumble, or a good punt return.

Later, after the forward pass was legalized, Yost emphasized pass defense as well. When the opponent made a mistake and turned over the ball, Michigan would attempt to capitalize swiftly, hoping by a fast touchdown or field goal to undermine the confidence of the other side. After 1906, when passing became a part of the game, Yost sought a good thrower to implement this strategy. The system became known as "a punt, a pass, and a prayer." It was not a crowd-pleasing style of play, with its almost passive dependence upon the opponent's mistakes. But it was a highly successful approach, yielding triumphs by the dozen, even after the great point-a-minute men graduated.

Yost's philosophy was evident in the first years too, but it tended to be overlooked because the offense was so astoundingly good at scoring touchdowns. The unstoppable Heston scored ninety-three of them in his four-season career. He played in forty-four games for Michigan, experiencing victory forty-three times and a deadlock once. The teams of 1901 and 1902 are generally considered to rank slightly above the later ones. Opponents usually sought to stop Heston, or his almost equally lethal halfback colleague, Albert Herrnstein, by jamming a nine-man line with two close backers. This would have worked against most offenses of the day, even the good ones. But Michigan, as might be expected of a team coached by a man who yelled "Hurry up!" all day long at practice, had more speed than anyone had ever seen before. Heston, or Herrnstein, or fullback Neil Snow would burst through the line and be gone almost before a linebacker could turn to pursue. With Heston, in particular, such pursuit was futile.

Throughout football history each great coach has had some technique, formation, or organizational nuance that gave his teams an advantage over the opposition. In the early days with Stagg and Warner it was new formations; with Rockne it was brilliant shifts, plays, psychological tricks, and an unmatched ability to instill spirit. With some, such as Gilmour Dobie at Cornell, Jock Sutherland at Pittsburgh, and Bernie Bierman at Minnesota, it was a consummate and painstaking attention to all the details of power blocking. Their teams literally ran opponents off the field. Finesse was not their forte, although occasional trick plays or passes were tried, in which case they nearly always worked because defenses

42

had been worn out trying to cope with their punishing ground attack.

With some coaches, such as Madison Bell at Southern Methodist, Wallace Butts at Georgia, Dutch Meyer at Texas Christian, or Glenn Dobbs at Tulsa, the aerial game took precedence, and their pass patterns were constructed with precisionlike skill. Pure inventiveness was the hallmark of such gifted men as Clark Shaughnessy at Stanford, who modernized the T formation; Don Faurot at Missouri, the originator of the split T; John McKay at Southern California, creator of the I formation; and David Nelson at Delaware, whose wing T formation was further refined with great success by his former Michigan teammate Forest Evashevski when the latter coached at Iowa. There have also been those highly imaginative coaches who have created entire offenses based upon deception and sleight of hand, such as Percy Haughton and Dick Harlow at Harvard, Fritz Crisler, first at Princeton, then at Michigan, Bobby Dodd at Georgia Tech, Francis Schmidt at Ohio State, Bob Zuppke at Illinois, and Andy Kerr at Colgate. Some have been great fundamentalists whose teams executed plays perfectly, such as Earl Blaik at Dartmouth and later West Point, Frank Leahy at Boston College and then Notre Dame, Bud Wilkinson at Oklahoma, Woody Hayes at Ohio State, Biggie Munn and Duffy Daugherty at Michigan State, and Darrell Royal at Texas. There have also been talented coaches whose inventiveness flowered in planning defenses. General Bob Neyland at Tennessee, Frank Thomas and Paul Bryant at Alabama, Wallace Wade at Duke, and Homer Norton at Texas A. & M. are but a few.

With Yost, however, the key to his immediate and unparalleled success was all in his nickname. The Hurry-Up Wolverines of 1901 were the talk of the country, gaining nearly 8,000 yards in their ten games. Willie Heston remembered that the team had a varied offense which included fifty-two well-rehearsed plays, all of them reeled off at breakneck speed. Most of the things a modern team does on offense, with the exception of the forward pass, were done by the point-a-minute teams. So it was only natural that Stanford, looking for a worthy opponent to inaugurate the Rose Bowl, would settle upon Michigan.

There had been flower parades for years in Pasadena, but the athletic activity had been confined mostly to foot races and bicycling. The football contest drew eight thousand curious spectators to Tournament Park. The Michigan players, enjoying the warm weather after having practiced in sub-zero temperatures at Ann Arbor, rode in one of the floats. Yost worried over the apparent sluggishness of his fourteen-man team, fearing that the Pasadena water and the warm weather would ennervate its 50-point-per-game offense. He did not rate the opponent as much of a threat, but this was a mistake, since the Westerners were well motivated.

For twenty-three minutes Stanford held valiantly against the onslaught of Michigan's whirling runners. Then, suddenly, a bit of deception broke the game open. Michigan worked a "naked reverse" which found ten men running in one direction, followed enthusiastically by eleven Stanford men, and Willie Heston traveling in the opposite direction, followed by no one at all. Oddly enough, it would be a quite similar maneuver by Columbia in the Rose Bowl game thirty-two years later which was to be responsible for another Stanford disaster in perhaps the biggest upset in postseason history.

Once the scoring parade began, it did not stop until Michigan had amassed 49 points. Stanford, by this time having none, and with the prospects for getting any beyond reasonable expectation, requested an end to hostilities. The Indians had run out of healthy players, and their walking wounded were sustained out of pride alone. Michigan, using no substitutes, had reeled off 20 plays good for 527 yards. The audience was completely convinced that here indeed was the football wonder of the world. If anyone had even suggested that Yost would send forth three more undefeated teams almost as devastating as this one, he would have been taken under a shade tree and sprinkled with cold water. Yet the squads of 1902, 1903, and 1904 would undoubtedly have done almost as well had they been invited to Pasadena. All four had the spark of Heston's running to power their offenses.

44

But there were no more invitations. The West had seen enough of Michigan, and the Tournament fathers in Pasadena had seen enough of football. For the next fourteen New Year's Days, chariot racing provided the entertainment. The first point-a-minute team had proved to be the thorn in the Rose Bowl.

5. End of an Era

Dr. Henry L. Williams looked up from his play diagrams one day on the Minnesota practice field and there was his old Yale classmate Pudge Heffelfinger. But Dr. Williams did not have too much time for pleasantries that cold afternoon in the autumn of 1903, much as he liked to pass the time with the immortal Pudge, for he was deep in thought over how to cope with the Michigan team which was coming to play at Northrup Field that Saturday. Heffelfinger understood his friend's concern, since he had observed Yost's seemingly invincible machine, now riding atop a twenty-nine-game winning streak. But Heffelfinger, as keen a football analyst as ever there was, thought he had discovered a way to contain the mercurial Heston and his almost equally dangerous cohorts. Where everyone else had presented a nine-man front with two backers, Heffelfinger suggested a seven-man defense, two linebackers, and two halfbacks as a final barrier. Heston and his friends would then have to breach three barricades, and that might slow them down just a bit. As novel as the plan was, however, it would not have posed much of a threat to Michigan if it had been executed by merely ordinary players. But Minnesota had in 1903 and again in 1904 two of the finest squads it would ever put on a football field. It took every bit of skill these extraordinary men had to cope with Yost's team, however, and the game was a landmark in the history of the gridiron.

It ended in a tie, 6–6. Each touchdown represented the only points registered against either team by an opponent all season. At the end of the year, each had eleven victories and a tie, with Michigan having scored 565 points and Minnesota 562. Seldom if ever in the annals of the sport have two teams with such imposing and, in fact, nearly identical records of conquest met during a season. One must think of Nebraska and Oklahoma in 1971, Notre Dame and Michigan State in 1966, Army and Notre Dame in 1946, or perhaps of Yale and Princeton in 1906 for a comparable example.

Heffelfinger's theory worked well enough to hold Heston to one touchdown when executed by the great Minnesota line, led by all-time stars Fred Schacht and Bobby Marshall. Heston admitted that it had been the most difficult afternoon of his career, although he did manage to gain over 100 yards. Indeed, it was the only time he ever walked off a gridiron at game's end without knowing the feeling of triumph. Minnesota, directed brilliantly by its quarterback, Sig Harris, outplayed the Wolverines, and Yost was glad to settle for a draw. He had never liked traveling, anyway, and this time he did something about the water. He brought Ann Arbor's own in several large earthenware jugs. In the confusion and ecstasy following the game—when Minnesota partisans, sensing a moral victory, swarmed over the field—someone neglected to pack one of the jugs. Oscar Munson, Minnesota's equipment custodian, came upon the abandoned vessel after everyone had departed. He took it to the locker room, got out a paint brush, and adorned it with the maroon and gold colors of the University of Minnesota, and, as an afterthought, painted upon it the score of the day's game. In huge letters it read: MINNESOTA 6; and in microscopic script: Michigan 6. Then Munson put the jug away in a cabinet and forgot all about it.

Thus was born the most celebrated trophy in the history of football, the Little Brown Jug. It was neither small nor beige, but it was Michigan's property, and Yost, when he realized that it was missing, wrote to Dr. Williams and asked for its return. Everyone at Minneapolis thought it would be a fine idea if Michigan came and got it the next time the two schools met on the gridiron. It took six years before another game was scheduled—and Michigan was then out of the Big Ten, by its own wish, in a complex dispute about regulations —but the Wolverines finally came and took the jug back. From then on, with only one hiatus, again tied to Michigan's dispute with the Western Conference, the two universities have contested with a vigor that borders upon frenzy for possession of an otherwise worthless piece of crockery.

The tie only served to ignite arguments during the rest of 1903 and all through 1904 over which was the better football team. Minnesota was just as high-scoring a club and practically as good on defense in 1904, but the real answer probably could be found in, of all places, Chicago. The University of Chicago teams, coached by the great Alonzo Stagg, were not on Minnesota's schedule during those seasons, but they were on Michigan's. Chicago was so good in 1902, 1903, and 1904 that it lost only four games, three of them to Michigan. In 1902 and 1904 the Wolverines were the only team to beat Stagg. It was largely on the basis of these triumphs over Chicago that Michigan's adherents felt their claim to superiority in the Midwest rested.

When the last weekend of the 1904 season rolled around, the Michigan partisans streamed into Ann Arbor and mingled with the loyal followers of Chicago to witness what everyone knew would be one of the great games of all time. Michigan's maize-and-blue banners had still not been lowered since Yost and Heston arrived, but now it was the great halfback's last game, and Stagg's undefeated Maroons thought that they finally had the power to compel the Wolverines to strike their colors. The main reason for their confidence was the presence of Walter Eckersall at quarterback. Eckersall possessed such a wealth of talent that an account of his accomplishments almost defies credulity. He is unanimously considered to have been the greatest quarterback of the pre-forward-pass era. Even Walter Camp, whose skepticism about non-Eastern players had been assuaged only by Heston, felt compelled to name Eckersall to three of his All-America teams.

On this storied afternoon Eckersall did not disappoint his followers; nor did Heston disenchant his. With Chicago's big, mobile linemen following his every movement and with the Maroon secondary closing in each time he got the ball,

Walter Eckersall of Chicago. All of the superlatives were justified.

the incomparable Michigan runner still managed to gain 248 yards to carry his team to victory. The score was 22–12. It was a tense, close, bitterly played affair, but Michigan was a shade better, and Heston was the difference. The one Chicago man he could not outshine, however, was Eckersall. Eckersall tackled Heston in the open field, from behind, which was an incredible feat. He also picked up a rare Heston fumble and ran it for a touchdown, just to remind the Michigan crowd that Chicago was still alive and kicking. But it was a hopeless gesture, and soon the game was over and Stagg was taking his men and his shattered hopes for an undefeated season back to the Midway. The Wolverines were still, after four years under Yost, the undefeated "Champions of the West."

The following year, with Heston an alumnus now embarked upon the legal career which would eventually put him on the bench (something no opponent could do), Midwestern coaches regarded the season with unaccustomed optimism. But the insatiable Wolverines proved them wrong and picked up right where they had left off. Yost still had an impregnable defense, bulwarked by the all-time linebacker Germany Schulz, and Michigan's offense, with little Norcross and the gifted Hammond brothers (who had been Eckersall's high school teammates at Hyde Park in Chicago), proved to be only a bit less productive than in the four previous years. So it was with an expectation bordering upon awe that the fans of the Midwest awaited the season's closing game at Marshall Field on the Midway between this seemingly invincible eleven and Stagg's Chicago.

In the forty-eight seasons in which it fielded a football team the University of Chicago never produced anything to equal its 1905 squad. It was a great coach's finest creation. With Eckersall at the throttle and with linemen such as Captain Mark Catlin and Arthur Badenoch, and the crushing Hugo Bezdek at fullback, the Maroons were the ones, if any mere humans could, to stop the Michigan Juggernaut.

More than 25,000 fans saw the clash on Thanksgiving Day, the biggest crowd the Midwest had ever seen. Chicago brought nine straight victories and a point score of 243 to its opponents' 5. Surely this was an impressive record, considering the high caliber of the competition the Maroons had engaged.

Yet no one could blame the Michigan partisans—who roared their allegiance to Yost's men—for being unconcerned. The Michigan team had extended its incredible undefeated streak to fifty-six games, fifty of them shutouts. It numbered twelve consecutive victims during the season, all of them held scoreless, while the Wolverines themselves had amassed 495 points. But for five years the sins of hubris had been mounting at Ann Arbor until now they weighed like an alp upon the Michigan men. And the gods, as is their wont, were about to bring forth nemesis.

It happened toward the end of a game which saw two perfectly matched machines battle each other to an almost complete stalemate. Strength countered strength, and there were few if any weaknesses to be exploited on either side. But when Dennie Clark of Michigan tried to run one of Eckersall's punts out of the end zone, Catlin and Badenoch of the Maroons succeeded in throwing him behind the goal for a safety. It had been a gamble on Clark's part, and if he had eluded the flying Chicago linemen, he might have traveled half the length of the field. Moreover, he was merely attempting a maneuver similar to one Eckersall had worked earlier when forced to punt from behind his own goal. Then the brilliant quarterback, fearing that a blocked kick would give Michigan a touchdown and that a short one would set up position for a field goal, faked the punt and ran around the surprised Wolverine defense. He did not go all the way but he did get the ball out of danger, and the next time he had to punt, it was from midfield and to the unfortunate Clark.

The 2–0 score stood up for the remaining few minutes, and a delirious Chicago crowned its own "Champions of the West" (and, in most experts' ratings, of the nation as well). Michigan had at long last been defeated, and an era had passed into football history. Ring Lardner perhaps best expressed the feelings of all the dispirited wearers of the Maize and Blue when he wrote that it was the first time his girl had ever seen him cry.

6. Teddy Lays Down the Law

In the East during these years just after the turn of the century, the old kings of the gridiron were still very much alive. It was true that some of the glamor of the game had moved westward to upstart places like Ann Arbor, Chicago, Minneapolis, and Madison, but there was still great prestige riding on the outcome of the annual confrontations in Cambridge, New Haven, and Princeton. In fact, there was little doubt that as a section the East was still the dominant force in the sport. When Harvard and Yale collided at the end of 1901, each carried an undefeated record into the action. Harvard emerged with a convincing 22–0 victory and a perfect season, and there were a great many students of the game who felt that the Crimson could have more than held its own against even Yost's mighty Michigan of that year.

The next year the script was exactly the opposite, as Yale, led by its great linemen Tom Shevlin, James Hogan, and Edgar Glass, ended Harvard's victory streak and earned itself an undefeated campaign by a score of 23–0. No one could tell the joyous New Haven throngs that there was an equal to the Bulldogs in all the land. They had, after all, stopped an undefeated, untied Harvard eleven cold. Yale's confidence knew no bounds, nor did anything happen all through the next season to shake it—that is, until the last game of the year. Then seemingly from out of nowhere came an inspired Princeton club whose rock-ribbed defense had shut out ten straight opponents. Yale managed to cross the hitherto unscathed Tiger goal, but it was not enough. Princeton won

11–6 and claimed both the Eastern and national championships. The two titans of the Midwest—Michigan and Minnesota—having tied each other, also demanded recognition. As always, there was no final arbiter, and the argument wore on until 1904.

Nobody in the East during these years, with the possible exception of Pennsylvania, had put together anything like the dynasty that Yost had created at Ann Arbor. And Pennsylvania had to labor under the suspicion that it was ducking games with Harvard, Yale, and Princeton. If a team wanted to be recognized as an undisputed sectional champion, it had to meet the best in its area, and Pennsylvania could not—or did not choose to—satisfy this requirement. The Penn boosters did point out, however, that their team was playing Pop Warner's always-tough Carlisle when the other powers were shying away from the Indians. But there was no getting away from the fact that to be top dog in the East in those years a team had to beat Yale and Princeton, just as it had to beat Michigan and Chicago if it wanted to be called the best in the Midwest.

Pennsylvania carved out a 12–0–0 record in 1904, scoring 222 points and holding opponents to a field goal. Yale won ten straight the following season with a similar scoring mark of 227 points, and allowing, likewise, only a field goal to the opposition. But in both years there was a strong challenge from the Midwestern schools for national attention.

In 1905, however, while Yale and Chicago were matching nearly identical records and clamoring for recognition from the nation's fans, there occurred a game which was to have a more lasting effect on the sport than perhaps any other.

Pennsylvania, in defeating Swarthmore that season, had concentrated its attack on the opponent's strongest man, following the well-proved theory that if one beats the best, the other players will lose heart. It worked well enough, and Penn won in a fierce, although legal, onslaught. But a photographer chanced to capture on film Bob Maxwell, the Swarthmore star, as he stumbled from the field, and the sight was almost enough to make strong men weep. It made one such man do more than that, however. President Theodore Roosevelt saw it and flew into a rage. It was not that the ebullient Teddy disliked the game. On the contrary, he had wanted very much to play for Harvard when he was a student there in the early eighties. Nor could he have been called a man overly sickened by violence. After all, he had been there at San Juan Hill during the Spanish-American police action a few years before and had even written some especially blood-curdling and obscenely chauvinistic descriptions of his part in the atrocity. Yet here he was, out of his head about the way football was being played. But, strangely, he was on the right track this time. This paradox of a man, who seemed on the one hand to revel in gore and yet was to win a Nobel Peace Prize, laid down the law, literally, to the fathers of football. Either they would legislate some order to the mayhem on the gridiron, or he would ban the game by Presidential edict.

The elder statesmen of football, led, as always, by Walter Camp, did not have to be told twice. All of them knew that when a season saw eighteen deaths and more than one hundred serious injuries, when schools such as Columbia and Northwestern dropped football altogether, and California and Stanford switched to Rugby, something was indeed wrong. They met and enacted far-reaching reforms which restructured the game into approximately what it is today. The major change was the legalization of the forward pass. Other refinements limited massed interference, established a neutral zone at the line of scrimmage, and increased the first-down yardage requirement from 5 in three tries to 10 in four.

It was the introduction of the forward pass, however, which changed the game more than any other single innovation since Camp had lifted it out of the Rugby category. Defenses from now on could not afford to crowd the line of scrimmage, since there was always the chance that some daredevil of a quarterback would fling the ball over their heads. The ball, of course, was still not shaped for the passing game. It was nearly round at the ends, made more for drop-kicking than for throwing. But as the years passed, the football evolved to suit the passers, who, to the surprise of no one, became the glamour boys of the gridiron.

54   *Bob Maxwell of Swarthmore (arrow) being pummeled*
by a trio of ill-mannered Pennsylvanians
in 1905. When he came off the field Maxwell
was a mess. Teddy saw the picture and football
got the message.

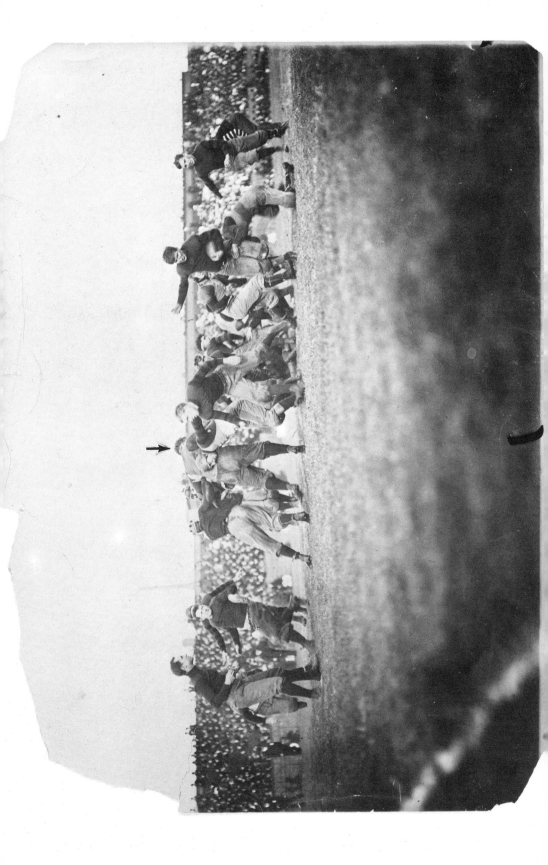

As with any really revolutionary development, it took some time before coaches could assimilate it into their game plans. One who was well ahead of his time was Eddie Cochems of St. Louis University. Cochems, a former end at Wisconsin, had been experimenting with passes in practice even before the legalization. In 1906 his strong team swept all opponents aside with a deft aerial game as the cornerstone of its offense. But St. Louis University, however good in its own league, was still not in the big time, and the real acceptance of the forward pass was nearly a decade in the future.

When Princeton and Yale met to decide the national championship in 1906, it was a brutal running game and an unyielding defense that rested at the core of each team's perfect record. Princeton had allowed but 9 points, Yale only 6. Neither had been a high-scoring club, and, as might have been expected, they bounced off each other with no points and a great many deep bruises to show for a furious afternoon's butting. Princeton claimed the title, but Yale men kept silent until the following week because they had a date with an undefeated Harvard team, which Princeton had somehow managed not to play that season. Yale came out with a hard-earned 6–0 victory, and all the Old Blues knew in their hearts who was king of the conquered East.

One thing the East lacked, however, was a really colorful and long-tenured coach. It had, for all its tradition and great teams, no Stagg, no Yost, and no Henry Williams. The only man who measured up to that trio was the prematurely nick-named "Pop" Warner (not yet forty), who guided Carlisle. In all the history of the game only Stagg could match him for innovations, and, if the truth be known, Warner was probably even more audacious in his concepts than the Grand Old Man.

Warner was a graduate of Cornell, where he had played guard in the nineties, boxed as a heavyweight, and earned a law degree. After brief coaching stints at his alma mater and Georgia, he had come to the tiny Carlisle Indian School in Pennsylvania. What he did there was akin to a coaching miracle. With a varsity that often included mere boys, he challenged the best teams in the country. His squads traveled

56

Glenn Scobey "Pop" Warner of Carlisle, Pittsburgh, and Stanford. He invented everything, it almost seemed, except the ball.

to all of the big-time campuses, delighting the fans and confounding the opposition with a fast, deceptive style of play. In 1907, before the immortal Jim Thorpe came upon the scene, Warner turned out one of his best teams. Carlisle handed Pennsylvania its only defeat of the season, by a decisive 26–6 score, and lost only one game itself, to a tough Princeton club. And was that enough to make the Tigers champion? It was not, for Princeton dropped a heartbreaker to Yale, and the Elis were alone once again atop the Eastern scramble.

The famous schools of the East had usually been coached by graduated captains of the previous season, or sometimes by a professional who stayed for only a few years. The first real coaching giant to break this tradition would arrive at Cambridge in 1908 to give not only Harvard its greatest succession of winning elevens, but American football its finest demonstration of applied science. He was a former Harvard lineman named Percy D. Haughton, and there are many students of the game who still believe that he was the most intelligent coach who ever stepped on a gridiron.

57

7. Haughton of Harvard

The head football coach at a big university today could probably pass for a chairman of the board or a chief of staff. With the game having become so vastly complicated and with assistants often numbering a dozen or more, the head man's principal task now is one of organization and grand strategy. Percy Haughton was not the first coach to apply the techniques of an efficiency expert to the game of football, but he was so extraordinarily successful at it that his nine-year accomplishment is all but unmatched. Certainly Harvard had never seen anything like him, nor has it since, and the same probably could be said of all the old schools of the East.

Haughton's Crimson teams won 71 games and lost only 7 against the best competition of the day. The East still had the strongest group of squads, collectively, in the nation and would retain this distinction until after the First World War. To go through an Eastern schedule with the kind of mark that Harvard established was undoubtedly the neatest trick of the decade.

Offensively, Haughton's teams presented a blend of speed, deception, and power that had seldom if ever been equaled. On defense, exhibiting unparalleled line play, they were nearly impossible to score against. In his attention to detail Haughton was like a human computer, and his merciless efficiency inevitably carried over into his relationships with his players. Everyone stood in awe of Haughton's cerebral skills and dedication, but his athletes seldom responded emotionally to him the way others did to Rockne, Stagg, or Zuppke.

Haughton had little of Rockne's wit and charm, Stagg's commanding moral presence, or Zuppke's blend of insight, contemplation, and humor. But he could do what ten thousand men of Harvard most wanted done: he could beat Yale.

His first Harvard team went through undefeated, although tied by Navy, and ruined Yale's season with a field goal. Only 8 points were registered against the Crimson all year. When Pennsylvania claimed the national championship on the basis of eleven victories and a tie with Carlisle, angry Cantabridgians retorted that a team which had not played any of the big three did not deserve such recognition. But Penn's backers pointed to a convincing win over previously undefeated Cornell, and a 29–0 rout of Michigan, which would stand as the worst defeat in Yost's twenty-five-year career at Ann Arbor. And even Harvard men had to concede that the Quakers' "Wild Bill" Hollenback was a line plunger who ranked with the best of them all.

Harvard was turning out great players of its own too that season, with Hamilton Fish and Charles Nourse leading the charge, and Wayland Minot and Hamilton Corbett running for daylight. In the next few years, moreover, Haughton would turn out such gifted linemen as Bob Fisher, Percy Wendell, and Stan Pennock to clear the path for all-time backfield stars Eddie Mahan and Charlie Brickley.

But just when it looked as though nothing could stop the Crimson from supplanting Yale as the dominant power in football, the old king in New Haven stirred mightily once more and the Blue produced perhaps its greatest team ever.

It took something that good to stop the Harvards of 1909, but Yale, under alumnus Howard Harding Jones, had so many heroes that Camp's All-America that year seemed to begin and end in New Haven. John Reed Kilpatrick at end, Henry Hobbs at tackle, Hamlin Andrus at guard, Carroll Cooney at center, and Steve Philbin and Ted Coy in the backfield were honored. Coy, in particular, was the one the Old Blues worshiped. He was to Yale what Heston was to Michigan, or Eckersall to Chicago, or what Thorpe would be to Carlisle.

The game between Harvard and Yale represented the last

time, until 1968, that they would enter with perfect records. It displayed two such excellent teams that for once there would be no argument as to a mythical national championship for the winner.

Harvard kept Yale from crossing its goal line but it could not stop Coy from making two long dropkicks, in those days worth four points each. The Crimson, in common with all of Yale's other opponents during the season, could not score, and the victory went to the Bulldogs, 8–0. Thus Yale finished its season with ten consecutive victories and a point total of 209 to 0. Some Yale men rate the 1923 team as the best the school ever fielded, while others extol the virtues of the 1960 perfect-record club on the theory that any modern team could have beaten the old-timers. But those who actually saw the 1909 champions in action seem almost awestruck in their descriptions, and it is safe to assume that the Blue never sent out a better eleven.

There was one other considerable accomplishment that season in which Michigan defeated both previously unbeaten Pennsylvania and Minnesota on their home fields on successive Saturdays. Yost no longer had high-scoring teams, but he still put out superb defensive units, and in 6'5", 270-pound Albert Benbrook he had the biggest, as well as the best, guard in the country.

Michigan had managed to get itself upset by Notre Dame earlier in the season in what was an astounding surprise to the Midwest and the first really big victory for the unheralded South Bend school. The hero for the Irish was Red Miller, one of six in his family to play for Notre Dame. The Millers of Notre Dame, in fact, rank with the Poes of Princeton and the Wisterts of Michigan among the most renowned of football's families.

It was during these years that the teams of the South began to attract attention. In 1904 three coaches had gone into Dixie bearing the newest strategies and techniques of the Northern leaders. Mike Donahue of Yale went to Auburn, John W. Heisman went from Pennsylvania to Georgia Tech, and Dan McGugin, one of Yost's point-a-minute team guards, set up shop at Vanderbilt. All enjoyed great success, with McGugin

60

bringing his Commodores to the front the most quickly and challenging Michigan, Harvard, and Yale. Vanderbilt began a long series with the Wolverines, during which it often came close but could not win. McGugin and Yost by this time had become brothers-in-law, having married sisters in Nashville. Both were also lawyers and both were to achieve a comparable Grand Old Man status at their respective universities. But try as they would, the Commodores could never get their deeply admired coach a victory over his alma mater. A tie in 1922 between otherwise all-victorious teams was the closest Vanderbilt ever got.

It was Heisman who would coach the first national breakthrough of a Southern team, winning universal acclaim during World War I on the crest of Georgia Tech's Golden Tornado.

But this was still far in the future. In 1909 football was going through another crisis of confidence. The introduction of the forward pass had not markedly reduced the brutality of the game, and all over the nation the cries of the injured were being drowned out by the clamor for reform. The toll for the year stood at thirty-three dead and over two hundred wounded. It reached the point where people began to suspect that war might be a less violent alternative to football, instead of the other way around, as the Harvard philosopher William James had suggested.

Once again the elder statesmen gathered and did for football what the Geneva Convention had done for warfare. Both the pushing and pulling of a ballcarrier were banned, as were blockers with arms interlocked and flying tackles. Seven men were required to be on the offensive line of scrimmage, thus further reducing the mass-momentum plays. The effect of the new rules was to bring the game even closer to the format observed today.

But new rules alone could not have pulled the game into the modern era. It was the forward pass, still regarded with suspicion and even disdain, which was about to accomplish this by making its long-overdue entrance on the national scene.

8. The Irish Arrive

There had been forward passes before that afternoon in 1913 on the plains of West Point when the upstarts from Notre Dame converted the East to the aerial game. In fact, there had even been a touchdown pass in a Yale–Princeton match several years earlier. But the Midwest was ahead of the East in its appreciation of the aerial game thanks largely to one of the classic encounters in history: the Minnesota–Michigan contest of 1910.

The Gopher eleven that rode into Ann Arbor for the season's finale had hammered out an incredible record of six consecutive victories against tough opponents without allowing any of them to score. Michigan, although unbeaten, had been tied three times and was not in a class with its rival—at least not on paper. Yost had determined that the only way to make any points against the huge Minnesota defense was to throw the ball. He had an end named Stanfield Wells, who was a more accurate passer than any of the backfield men, and a special play was worked out which would allow him to pitch the ball to his opposite end, Stanley Borleske.

On the Minnesota varsity that day was a substitute named Clark Shaughnessy. In later years he would become the originator of the modern, man-in-motion T formation, the offense that captured the fancy of nearly every other coach and now dominates the sport. Shaughnessy wrote, long after the game, that merely witnessing the Minnesota–Michigan affair of 1910 had convinced him to become a football coach.

Until well into the final quarter the two enormous lines,

each averaging more than 220 pounds per man, battled each other to a standstill. Then Michigan took the ball near midfield. Wells quickly retreated into the backfield and threw the ball as far as he could, in the general direction of Borleske. The play worked for a big gain and unnerved the Gophers. Wells and Borleske immediately collaborated again, and the ball was placed only a few yards from the goal. Wells was now moved from end to fullback, and the All-America nominee responded by driving over for the game's only touchdown. It was one of the most satisfying victories in Michigan's long and proud football history. A great Minnesota team had been thwarted by means of the forward pass, and the new weapon—which had not been appreciated in the Midwest except at St. Louis—now became the talk of the section.

Jack Marks, the former Dartmouth star who coached Notre Dame, had been impressed by Michigan's use of the pass. Marks stayed only two seasons at South Bend, but both of his teams were undefeated. When the much-admired Jesse Harper took his place in 1913, the ingredients were present on the Notre Dame varsity for a first-rate aerial game.

Harper had learned his football from the master, Alonzo Stagg, at Chicago. Now he determined to capitalize upon quarterback Gus Dorais's ability to throw accurately to his ends, especially to the one with the face of an unsuccessful prizefighter. Knute Kenneth Rockne, the immigrant boy from Voss, Norway, who had worked in the Chicago post office to save the money to enter Notre Dame, was even then a brilliant student of the game. He and Dorais had worked out a series of pass patterns and were waiting only for the right time to put them into play.

The propitious moment took place that autumn on the plains of West Point, where the Irish had gone as the guests of the Army's powerful eleven. It has remained a long-standing untruth that everyone in the East looked down upon Notre Dame. Most fans realized that although the Midwesterners were relatively unpublicized, they had still gone through two straight seasons without losing and had beaten some respectable foes.

Nevertheless, the football world in general, and the

Eastern province in particular, was astounded at the ease with which the Irish routed a good Army eleven. The score was 35–13, and the major damage was done through the air lanes in the second half, as Dorais found nothing but holes in the Cadet pass defense. It is said that even when Rockne made a mistake and fell down while running out for a pass, he turned it to Notre Dame's advantage. The opportunistic Norwegian merely picked himself up, whirled around to face Dorais, and received the ball. The Army defensive back, thinking that Rockne would continue running, was too far away to intervene. This may have been the origin of the "button hook" pass pattern, in which the receiver heads downfield at full speed, drawing the defensive back with him, then stops and quickly turns around to catch the ball.

For Army's partisans the defeat was mingled with the satisfaction of knowing that they had seen in two years two of the epic performances in the history of the game. The previous season Jim Thorpe had come up to West Point and put on a show that people would talk about for the rest of their lives. He all but single-handedly had accomplished the destruction of a strong Army team by a score of 27–6, and even the desperate efforts of such stalwarts as Prichard and Dwight David Eisenhower were fruitless. Over the course of the season Thorpe gained 1,869 yards rushing, and scored 224 points on 29 touchdowns, 38 extra points, and 4 field goals.

So much has been written about the incomparable Thorpe that further repetition of his exploits is superfluous. It is enough to say that probably a majority of the students of the game think that he was its greatest player. Arguments will always rage over who was the top running back, whether it was Heston, Coy, Mahan, Grange, Harley, Berwanger, Nagurski, Harmon, Cagle, Matson, Davis, Blanchard, Walker, Brown, Simpson, or some other. And each famous passer, too, has his acolytes, who sing the praises of Baston, Friedman, Oberlander, Howell, Baugh, O'Brien, Graham, Bertelli, Gilmer, Christman, Lujack, Allerdice, Chappuis, Kazmaier, Frank, Conerly, Rhome, Namath, Sinkwich, and many more. But the most impassioned disputes usually subside when Thorpe's

Jim Thorpe of Carlisle. One of the four in everybody's all-time backfield.

name is brought up. He is on nearly everybody's list as one of the four in the all-time backfield.

If the big Indian and his Carlisle teammates were the most spectacular club performing on the Eastern gridirons during those years, Haughton's Harvard was still the best. In 1912 and again in 1913 the Crimson swept to perfect seasons, and there was no doubt anywhere that they were the national champions. In 1912, in particular, Harvard knew the exquisite joy of ruining undefeated seasons for both Princeton and Yale. The following year Haughton's system was working just as well, and with its superb kicker, Charlie Brickley, scoring five field goals, Harvard eased past another fine Yale team.

Everything seemed to be going so inexorably according to Haughton's meticulous plans that Yale now turned in desperation to one of its immortals in an attempt to deflate mighty Harvard. Thus it was that, a generation after his heroic quadrennium as an All-America end, Frank Hinkey returned to New Haven as coach of his alma mater. When Yale men spoke of Hinkey, it was in the same hushed tones that they reserved only for the likes of Pudge Heffelfinger. These two were, perhaps more than any other ancient wearers of the Blue, the closest to the fictional Frank Merriwell, that legendary personification of the gods' refusal to let Yale lose.

When Hinkey played defensive end in the brutal flying-wedge era of the nineties, he never weighed more than 155 pounds, yet he was the best there ever was. He had come out of upstate New York—the Tonowanda Terror, they called him —to materialize one day on the Yale flank, a wraithlike figure who seemed suddenly to explode in the faces of opposing runners and to leave both them and their interference in total disarray.

His coaching style owed much to the then prevalent lateral-pass offense popularized by the Canadian universities. A variation of this technique was installed many years later by Andy Kerr at Colgate with gratifying results. Observers around the Yale practice field, however, were skeptical about Hinkey's theories. There was a great element of risk in the constant tossing of the ball backward to trailing runners. A clever defense could disrupt the attack, and the danger of fumbling

Percy Haughton of Harvard, with his field-goal kicker extraordinary, Charlie Brickley. Why shouldn't the best university have the best football team?

was great. But when Hinkey got his big chance to convince the doubters, in the Notre Dame game of 1914, the proficiency of the Yale movements surprised even him. For the Irish, who had come East with soaring expectations, it was a disaster. They were annihilated by a score of 28–0, and lost later in the year to Army, a more conventional but much sounder team than Yale.

By the time the Bulldogs went to challenge Haughton's awesome Harvard machine, they had won seven out of eight, losing only to Washington and Jefferson in an upset. What Harvard did to Hinkey's men, however, was something no mere mortals could have prevented. The Crimson, rolling to its third straight undefeated campaign, although having played ties with Penn State and Brown, destroyed Yale by a 36–0 margin. The Harvards could not believe it; the Yales did not want to.

Hinkey stayed another year at New Haven, hoping that conditions would improve, and certain that whatever else happened, he could not lose more ignominiously to Harvard again. He was wrong. The 1915 score was 41–0, and for a while it seemed as though the very concrete supports of the vast Yale Bowl, which had been erected the year before, were about to crumble.

Harvard in 1915 was bidding for a fourth consecutive undefeated season, and except for the greatest team that Cornell had thus far fielded, would have made it. When the two strongest elevens in the nation collided at midseason, it was a game to be savored by those who fancy the niceties of perfect fundamental football. The Big Red had opened the season with four easy games in preparation for what it knew would make or break its claim to the national championship. With the celebrated Charlie Barrett carrying the ball, and with inspired performances from such stalwarts as All-America end Murray Shelton and the aptly named Gib Cool, Cornell stopped Haughton's invincible team by a score of 10–0. It was the only subpar effort of Eddie Mahan's career, but it is doubtful that even a top-form showing by the Harvard hero could have thwarted Cornell. For years the team from Ithaca had been seated below the salt at the Eastern football ban-

Frank Hinkey, the Tonowanda Terror. To the Harvards and the Princetons, this was one bad Yalie.

quet. Now the Big Red moved dramatically to the head of the table. Michigan and Pennsylvania were disposed of with dispatch, and the Cornellians discovered that they liked very much to be number one. In a few years, when gloomy Gilmour Dobie would come out of the West, the faithful in Ithaca were to revel in a surfeit of such glories.

There was only one thing left for Haughton's chagrined men after the Cornell defeat and that was to assuage their frustration at the expense of Yale. This was easy, since the Elis were staggering to the end of an awful season. The 41–0 Harvard score might even have been worse had not Yale still retained a little pride. Her men fought gamely, but they were simply outclassed. If any Yale man had been so rash as to predict that one year later the Blue would stop Harvard cold, even denying it a touchdown, he would have been sent away for a long rest. But Haughton's remarkable cycle of triumph was winding to a close, and Yale was about to receive another alumnus, with the formidable name of Thomas Albert Dwight Jones, and his coaching accomplishments were to prove no less formidable.

70

9. "I Am Louis XIV"

The second decade of the twentieth century saw the beginning of football excellence at a number of universities which had previously attracted little notice. In the Midwest, Illinois and Ohio State produced their first sectional champions and saw their leading players attain nationwide prominence. In the South, Heisman constructed a dynasty at Georgia Tech, and soon the fans all over the country began to understand what the partisans along Peachtree Street had been cheering about for years.

In the West, where the leading schools, Stanford and California, had only just returned to the gridiron after their long excursion into Rugby, all the noise was coming from Seattle. There, in what had heretofore been a football backwater, a dour, moody, former Minnesota quarterback, Gilmour Dobie, produced nine consecutive undefeated teams in as many seasons at the University of Washington. Dobie then packed his bags and headed East, leaving with a record of 58 victories, 3 ties, and no defeats.

Critics, however, made the telling arguments that the caliber of the Huskies' opposition had been third-rate, that they had never gone against a good team from the more established sections of the country, and that a distressing number of their triumphs had been at the expense of high school teams and the crews of naval vessels anchored in Seattle harbor. But Dobie would later convince most of the skeptics with almost equally impressive statistics—at least in his first years—at Cornell, where the competition was much better.

71

Coach Gilmour Dobie. As close as he ever came to smiling.

His punishing, old-fashioned offense placed great emphasis on a bulldozing ground attack featuring a few flawlessly executed plays. Dobie's teams disdained the passing game, and this cost them heavily after other coaches conjured up successful defenses against their running plays. But Dobie, as might have been expected of an old Minnesota quarterback, never considered passing to be real football.

The new coach down at Champaign in 1913 did, however. He was aware of all the new trends in the game, probably because he had helped to create so many himself. His name was Robert Carl Zuppke, and after he had tutored just two Illinois teams, all the wearers of the Orange and Blue knew that they had found themselves one of the real geniuses of the game.

72

Zuppke was a graduate of Wisconsin, where he had been too small for anything except the scrub team. But perhaps not being on the field had enabled him to see football with a creative overview that was denied to those in the scrimmage. Zuppke's teams, whatever their record, always glittered with offensive specialties. They were light, fast, deft in ball handling, and devastatingly opportunistic. Zuppke spent hours devising new plays, such as the famous "flea-flicker," in which an end takes a quick pass from the quarterback and then laterals the ball to a trailing halfback almost in one movement. It won a number of games for the Illini during the twenty-nine years that Zuppke coached.

In common with many inventive men, Zuppke was a complex person. He had gone to New York after college, hoping to become a painter. He gave his artistic inclinations a bohemian fling and then, realizing that the auguries were not favorable, returned to the Midwest to pursue a more mundane life. But his talent with a brush was to win him recognition of a sort in later years after he had attained fame as a coach. He became known as the "Rembrandt of the prairies," and exhibited many of his canvasses. Zuppke was also interested in other areas of culture. He read deeply in philosophy, devouring the works of the ancient Greeks and the modern Germans, becoming an especially dedicated student of Schopenhauer and Kant. All in all, it was an unusual background for one of the most successful of football coaches. In this many-sided man there also were combined to an equally unusual degree the gifts of a psychologist, a raconteur, and a self-deprecating humorist. The blend made Bob Zuppke not only one of the most admired coaches in all the history of the game, but one of the very few who was genuinely liked as well. Most biographies of coaches descend to meaningless repetition by describing one and all as having been beloved, or adored, or worshiped, when, in reality, many inspired just the opposite emotions. Once in a while, however, there emerged a rare leader who deserved the superlatives, and Zuppke is almost unanimously felt to have been one of these.

His second Illinois team was undoubtedly one of the best the Midwest had seen. It swept aside seven opponents, scor-

Robert Carl Zuppke of Illinois. Schopenhauer, Kant, the oils, and the "flea flicker"—all in one lifetime.

ing 224 points against 22, and experiencing difficulties only with Minnesota and Chicago. The 1914 Illini had dazzling backfield stars—such as Harold Pogue, Potsy Clark, and Bart Macomber—running and passing behind a line led by Ralph Chapman and Perry Graves. Defensively, they were chillingly proficient at turning opponents' errors into Illinois touchdowns, one of the hallmarks of any superior team. In Pogue the Orange and Blue had a runner who lacked breakaway speed and, at 150 pounds, was devoid of heft yet somehow managed to make the big play. He had an uncanny way of sifting through enemy defenses, and a sixth sense in avoiding tacklers. In later years Zuppke noted that his other Harold—Grange—ran much as Pogue had, only faster. To augment Pogue's talents, which were often displayed for half a game in deference to his frailty, Illinois could call on the astute Clark, who fulfilled completely Zuppke's vision of the perfect quarterback. It was little wonder, then, that the Midwestern faithful, after watching these athletes, turned a deaf ear to the Eastern contention that either Harvard's or Army's unbeaten elevens were the nation's best.

Illinois remained undefeated, although tied, the following season. Then its fortunes declined. The 1916 squad was but a shell of the championship clubs, although Macomber had continued his improvement from game to game and emerged as a great star. Zuppke's troubles multiplied until one week they all seemed to coalesce. His lackluster charges had to face Minnesota, and the prospect was one to induce withdrawal symptoms even in a bunch of extroverts.

Just a look at the points Minnesota had amassed in its first four games—236—was enough to awe the Illini. It was true that three victims had been small-time teams from the Dakotas, but on the previous Saturday the Gophers had left Iowa for dead by an unbelievable margin of 67–0. The Iowa coach, the same Howard Harding Jones who had taught the great Yale team of 1909, went away mumbling to himself about having seen the most terrifying football machine of the age. Indeed, Jones was not alone in his appraisal. Dr. Williams' Gophers had convinced numerous experts that they were the Perfect Team, and that is what they were now being called in the newspapers. Minnesota seemed to have no real weakness. It had a strong and agile line, crushing runners, and the best passing combination of the year in Pudge Wyman throwing to All-America end Bert Baston.

All Zuppke knew about the Gophers was that they used the same three-play running sequence to open each game and that the maneuvers usually worked for huge gains. He set his defenses to stop these plays, taking the chance that Minnesota might try something else. He also devised a spread offense in which the Illini would deploy all across the gridiron. From this alignment Macomber would throw passes to his excellent halfback Dutch Sternaman.

After he had made these plans, Zuppke sat back and let psychology work its ways. He constantly praised Minnesota to his players, had them pore over the bushels of newspaper clippings predicting their demise, and finally told them to enjoy themselves and not to worry about the outcome. "I am Louis XIV," Zuppke told the uncomprehending Illini, "and you are my court. After us the deluge."

The Gophers were so confident of victory that they designed a special visitor's box and invited Walter Camp to view the game and make his All-America selections from the Minnesota varsity.

Ring Lardner, who knew a lot about football, wrote that Illinois would achieve a moral victory if it could hold the Gophers to fewer than 49 points. If some charitably inefficient linotypist had only managed to omit the "4," Lardner would have qualified as the reincarnation of Nostradamus. The Illini not only held Minnesota to 9 points, they scored 14 themselves in achieving one of the two or three greatest upsets in the annals of football.

Zuppke's strategy on both offense and defense worked perfectly. Illinois stopped the first three Minnesota plays cold, shaking the host team's confidence at the very outset. Once in possession of the ball themselves, Macomber and Sternaman worked their passing maneuvers out of the spread formation, which added confusion to Minnesota's other discomfort. A quick touchdown resulted, but the game was still young when Minnesota took the ensuing kickoff. Wyman went for a quick equalizer, and it was then that disaster struck the Gophers. His aerial went awry and into the hands of Ren Kraft of Illinois, who carried it 50 yards for a touchdown. Now Minnesota trailed 14–0 after only a few minutes, and consternation gave way to despair.

For the rest of the afternoon Illinois grimly hung on, thwarting one Minnesota drive after another. The favorites did push across 9 points, but at the crucial moments they faltered. A last-minute pass was again intercepted and the upset preserved.

As an indication of the power of the Minnesota team, it won the two remaining games on its schedule by scores of 54–0 over Wisconsin and 49–0 over Stagg's Chicago, both good elevens. Dr. Williams thought, at the end of his career, that this team had been the best of his twenty-two, in spite of the defeat. It was undoubtedly the strongest in the Big Ten, but it did not win the championship.

That distinction went to Ohio State University, which had joined the conference only four years earlier. Ohio State, under Dr. John W. Wilce, a distinguished medical researcher, made its grand entrance on the national scene with an undefeated team. Its key player, and the man who after more than half a century is still the most revered figure in Buckeye football history, was Charles Wesley Harley.

"Chic" Harley, as his fellow townsman and Ohio State alumnus, James Thurber, later wrote, was the center of life in Columbus during the years from 1916 until 1919. Harley was a hometown boy who had played high school football almost in the shadow of Ohio Field. He had accumulated an enormous group of admirers in Columbus even before he appeared in a college game. A perfectly coordinated runner, passer, and kicker, Harley had the ability, which all great players have, of achieving his best in the most important games. In 1917 he again led the Buckeyes to an undefeated season. But in his final year, after the war, Harley experienced the only defeat of his career. In the fourth quarter of the last game of 1919, with the Buckeyes leading Illinois by a point and needing only to retain possession of the ball in order to win the Big Ten title, Harley tried a pass and suffered a

John W. Heisman of Georgia Tech. A trophy, a Tornado, and here, a toast.

disastrous interception. Illinois then moved into field-goal range, Bob Fletcher kicked perfectly, and the Ohio State faithful were reduced, as Thurber remembered it, to a most pitiable condition.

Harley was named to the All-America team twice, thus becoming the first from Ohio State to be honored. Walter Camp selected him as a sophomore, which was all the more amazing, since Camp had reservations about sophomores in general and about those at the lesser known Midwestern schools in particular.

It had been observed, for example, by partisans of Purdue that their hero, Elmer Oliphant, had received his undoubtedly justified recognition only after he played at West Point. Oliphant, an athlete of varsity caliber in seven different sports, was universally acknowledged to be an all-time star on the gridiron. He led Army to a perfect season in 1916, the last such accomplishment for the Cadets until 1944.

Army men thought they had the nation's best team in 1916, but most experts favored the University of Pittsburgh, coached by Pop Warner, who had moved from Carlisle. Warner turned out perfect-record elevens in 1915, 1916, and 1917. There were players on these teams who went through their entire varsity careers without knowing either defeat or tie. In the years since, only the men of Cornell in 1921–22–23 and Oklahoma in 1954–55–56 have known a comparable feeling.

Warner's teams were unyielding on defense, led by the undersized but furiously active center Bob Peck, a rare three-time All-America selection. At tackle was John Bain Sutherland, who later took a degree in dentistry, turned to coaching, and from 1924 through 1938 made Pitt a national byword for power football.

The Panthers had good backfields, and a top performer in George McLaren. They won most of their games with ease, but complaints were heard about the schedule, which was largely made up of in-state opponents. There were, of course, some very strong teams playing in Pennsylvania then. In those years Washington and Jefferson and Carnegie Tech were powerful, as were Penn State and the traditional leader, Pennsylvania. Pitt played and defeated these opponents. Victories over good Navy and Syracuse teams were also recorded.

But people wondered how Pitt would have done, for example, if it had got in the way of Heisman's Golden Tornado from Georgia Tech. The Engineers, everyone who saw them agreed, were the best team yet to come out of the South. They also had the distinction of running up the biggest score in the history of football, 222–0, over Cumberland. In this game, Cumberland made a number of mistakes, the principal one being to show up in the first place.

In 1917 Heisman, knowing that the only way to win the national recognition he so desperately wanted was to beat a big Eastern team, scheduled a game with his alma mater, Pennsylvania. Pitt also played Penn that year and had trouble winning by a touchdown. Georgia Tech, however, working out of a tricky shift, and with luminaries such as George Strupper, and Joe Guyon in top form, annihilated the Red and Blue by a score of 41–0. The East was convinced. The Midwest had to wait a few weeks until Auburn—which had held unbeaten

Big Ten champion Ohio State to a scoreless tie—went against Tech. The score was 68–7 in Georgia Tech's favor, and the first Southern team to claim a national championship had convinced just about everyone that the rating was entirely proper.

Only in Pittsburgh was there disagreement. Despite the inconvenience of the First World War, Warner and Heisman agreed to match what was left of their teams the following season. Warner thought that he had solved the riddle of the Tech shift and was proved correct when Pitt outclassed the Engineers 32–0.

The war, however, had largely diminished the importance of football games, and a number of schools abandoned the sport during 1918.

10. An Age of Heroes

The time in American history between the armistice and the crash still glows, even in the perspective of a half century, with an almost mesmerizing intensity. These years witnessed a peculiar conjunction of prohibition, disillusion, literary creativity, political stagnation, and ethical myopia. Babbitt and bohemia struggled for possession of the national soul against a backdrop of fragmenting traditions and an unprecedented flourishing of the colorful, the zany, and the bizarre.

No other period has called forth so many aliases: the Roaring Twenties, the Golden Twenties, the Dry Decade, the Era of Excess, the Era of Wonderful Nonsense, the Jazz Age. It was the last big spree, marking a national rite of passage, a maudlin farewell to the innocence and hope of a childhood now irrevocably gone. And it was more than just a coincidence that when this age found its poet, F. Scott Fitzgerald would write longingly of the pads worn for a day on the football fields of Princeton.

An age in quest of heroes looked to the gridiron and saw Rockne and Gipp, the Galloping Ghost and the Four Horsemen, Wrong-Way Riegels, Friedman and Oosterbaan, Wonder Teams, Devine Teams, Praying Colonels, the Team of Destiny, Ramblers and Nomads, Nagurski and Nevers, Kaw and Pfann, Red Cagle and Little Boy Blue. The country went wild over them all. A football mania never equaled since swept the land, accompanied by the hip flask, the raccoon coat, and the Stutz Bearcat.

The faithful came in such numbers that vast concrete

ovals had to be reared to accommodate them. In football-mad Columbus, Ohio State opened its immense horseshoe in 1922, followed soon by Illinois and then by Michigan, which scooped out the top of a hill and filled it with 87,000 seats—successively enlarged over the years to 101,001—the biggest college-owned saucer of them all.

The team everybody wanted to see was Notre Dame, and the name on everybody's lips was Rockne—the same Rockne who had caught Gus Dorais's passes that afternoon in 1913 on the plains of West Point when the Irish burst upon the national scene.

From this point on, Notre Dame and the gridiron were to become synonymous. No other school can match the small men's college in South Bend in the matter of dominance over the sport of football. And it is to Rockne more than to any other of its celebrated alumni that Notre Dame owes this distinction.

Rockne was not an inventive genius of the caliber of Stagg or Pop Warner. Nor could he match the encyclopedic knowledge and strategic brilliance of a Yost or a Haughton, but he had something that none of those great coaches had: he most profoundly understood and reflected his times, and appreciated fully the importance of the institutions of mass communication. In addition, he was a resourceful coach, capable of an eclectic gathering of the best in other systems and always willing to acknowledge a debt to the old masters. For example, he freely admitted that he had incorporated many of the techniques of his predecessor, Jesse Harper, noting that Harper had imbibed his tactical theories as one of Stagg's players at Chicago.

Rockne possessed dedication, insight, wit, and humor. That most overworked of words "charisma," which applies to only a few men, would be an exact appraisal of his effect upon his players. In common with many of the best of the old-time coaches, Rockne had a many-faceted intelligence. He was a superb chemist and could just as easily have matched his brilliant coaching record with accomplishments in the laboratory. It is interesting to note that Yost, McGugin, and Warner had law degrees, Williams and Wilce doctorates in medicine

Knute Rockne of Notre Dame. It began   83
in a Norwegian village. It ended in a
Kansas wheatfield. And in between,
a legend was born.

George Gipp of Notre Dame. "Good luck," the Gipper wished us all, and then he died at twenty-five of a strep throat. But in the process, he became an immortal.

and distinguished research achievements, Sutherland a dental career and a lectureship at Pittsburgh, and Zuppke all the gifts of a philosophy professor, although without a formal chair in the subject. Moreover, coaches such as Stagg, Haughton, the Jones brothers—Howard and Tad—Dobie, and Jesse Hawley of Dartmouth were men of demonstrated intellect in areas apart from football.

These were only typical of the game's early teachers. In modern times the job of the head coach has become so complex that it is a rare man who has the cerebral energy to master another profession. This is not to argue, however, that the ancients were any wiser. The open-minded modern coach may actually be much more knowledgeable about the behavioral currents of his times. A coach today who has made the considerable mental effort to understand athletes—not merely as performers but as often-troubled inhabitants of a perplexing age—must demonstrate the skills of a social scientist, not to mention those of a psychiatrist as well.

For Rockne, in his first years under the Golden Dome at South Bend, there was a twofold problem: he had to win games and also to improve the caliber of Notre Dame's schedule. The Irish had been largely ignored by most Big Ten schools. Some said that this was owing to religious intolerance, but whatever the truth of the contention, the fact was that Notre Dame was forced to look to other sections for its opponents. When Rockne's 1919 and 1920 teams went unbeaten, they faced relatively undemanding schedules, but by the time his career was at its height, Notre Dame was playing many of the best teams in the country.

The squads of 1919 and 1920 were led by George Gipp, who has since become a legend at Notre Dame. Nearly all football fans know the tale of Gipp's deathbed request to Rockne and the fulfillment of that plea years later when a weak Irish eleven upset the Army in 1928. "Win one for the Gipper" remains one of the enduring battle cries of the game, but it does not require that Gipp be canonized to ensure his fame. In fact, he was something less than a choirboy, being an extremely bright but cynical hustler who laughed at Rockne's training rules and even wagered money on the games. The investments were of the low-risk variety while Gipp was on the field. He ran, passed, blocked, and defended better than any player Rockne ever coached and is still considered Notre Dame's all-time star.

It took a lot more than just Gipp, however, to ensure the success of Rockne's early teams. The main reason they were running away from their opponents was the perfectly timed shift which their coach had installed. Notre Dame would line up in a T formation, then jump into its famous "box." Before the opponent could adjust its defense, the Irish were off and running. The shift was even better than the one Dr. Henry Williams had worked out at Minnesota.

There was such a chorus of protest from defeated coaches that the rules makers continually legislated restrictions on the Notre Dame shift. Rockne raged at this persecution, but he knew that the material was so good and so well motivated by his psychological skill that he could win with any system. His gimmicks merely made the game more exciting for the spectators. Because of Rockne and his early success, Notre Dame found itself in the enviable position of being a magnet for aspiring football players. Many of them later carried Rockne's teachings into the coaching ranks. Rockne, in fact, turned out more future head coaches than anyone in the history of the game. They included Eddie Anderson at Holy Cross and Iowa, Frank Thomas at Alabama, Harry Mehre at Georgia, Buck Shaw at Santa Clara, Harry Stuhldreher at Villanova and Wisconsin, Jim Crowley at Michigan State and Fordham, and two who guided their alma mater, Elmer Layden and Frank Leahy. These were only the better known. There were dozens of others who went out to high schools all over the country, but never forgot their coach when it came to sending him their most promising prospects.

Thus, it seemed for a long time that nothing could stop Notre Dame, and except for the best team Iowa ever had, in 1921, and two inspired upsets by Nebraska in 1922 and 1923, nothing did. The next season the Four Horsemen put the finishing touches on a six-year cycle during which Rockne's teams lost only three games.

The Four Horsemen, the most famous backfield in foot-

The Four Horsemen of Notre Dame.
From left, Don Miller, Elmer Layden,
Jim Crowley, and Harry Stuhldreher.

ball history, were born in the Sunday sports pages of October 19, 1924. It was there that Grantland Rice's endlessly quoted lead introduced them to the public as the personification of the riders of the apocalypse. "Outlined against a blue-gray October sky," Rice wrote, "the Four Horsemen rode again. In dramatic lore they are known as Famine, Pestilence, Destruction, and Death. These are only aliases. Their real names are Stuhldreher, Miller, Crowley, and Layden."

The nation's most famous sportswriter then went on to record how the Irish had defeated an excellent Army team by a touchdown to keep their record perfect. The Horsemen were then seniors, having been vastly successful against every opponent during their first two seasons, except for the two upsets by Nebraska. Their major concern in 1924, therefore, was to make certain that the Cornhuskers did not ruin still a third undefeated year. It turned out that there was little to worry about, since Nebraska was brushed aside easily, as were good Princeton and Northwestern teams. Finishing with a perfect record, Rockne decided to accept Stanford's invitation to play in the Rose Bowl game. It was to be the final fling for the Horsemen and their unsung blockers in the line, who were given the less glamorous nickname the Seven Mules.

What made Rockne's backfield so good was its combination of speed and coordination. The four were all under 170 pounds, but each moved well and could run and pass. They took advantage of this amazing versatility by working multiple exchanges, laterals, and other deceptive maneuvers with consummate skill. Stuhldreher, at quarterback, was a highly intelligent tactician and the leading passer. Crowley and Miller had all the attributes of All-America halfbacks. Miller was another of the clan which would contribute star players to Notre Dame over a fifty-year span. At fullback, Elmer Layden seemed too frail at 165 pounds to crack an enemy line, but appearances were deceiving. He was a much better open-field runner than most fullbacks, moreover, because of his exceptional speed. All of the Horsemen were good on defense, with Layden shining particularly at pass interceptions.

Strangely, it was their defensive ability rather than their much-advertised offensive prowess which brought the Horsemen victory in the Rose Bowl. The game has been long remembered as one of the epics. It brought together the two most publicized coaches of the season, the two most widely emulated offensive styles, and several of the all-time greats of the gridiron. In addition, the national championship rode on the outcome.

Stanford had completed its regular schedule undefeated, although tied by California. The tie, one of the most exciting ever played, constituted a moral victory for Stanford. The Indians were forced to play without their best back, Ernie Nevers, yet still managed to come from behind with two last-quarter touchdowns.

Nevers is Stanford's most celebrated football player and one of the best fullbacks in history. Pop Warner rated him above Thorpe as an all-round performer. In the Warner offense, Nevers handled the ball on nearly every play. He could pass and block, and he backed up the line with authority on defense, but it was as a ballcarrier that Nevers reached the supreme heights. He alone gained 114 yards against Notre Dame despite injured ankles, while the Horsemen combined advanced only 127 yards from scrimmage.

Nevers, however, suffered two catastrophic pass interceptions, both run back 70 yards for touchdowns by the alert Layden. The strategy of using flat passes against a team with Notre Dame's speed was questioned later by unhappy Stanford partisans. The Irish picked up a third touchdown on a fumbled punt and thus accounted for only one score on offense. Yet despite its costly mistakes, Stanford was still in the game late in the fourth quarter when Nevers carried the ball to the Notre Dame 1-yard line. A touchdown would have narrowed the Irish lead to only 3 points and given the heavier Stanford team an immense psychological lift. But Notre Dame braced and stopped the charging Nevers inches short of the goal on the crucial fourth down. An intense disagreement arose immediately, with the Stanford men claiming that he had scored, but the officials rejected the contention.

Notre Dame won the game 27–10, and Rockne was glad to be delivered from the tough Stanfords and their crushing fullback, but he could not agree with Pop Warner that the

losers were really a better team. Warner based his feeling on that fact that Stanford had contained the Horsemen on offense, while Nevers had shredded the Notre Dame defense. But alertness to an opponent's mistakes has always been the hallmark of a great team, and to win, despite being outplayed at the scrimmage line, stamped the Irish as a worthy champion.

With the big names having been graduated, Notre Dame stumbled in 1925, then came back strongly the next year. Only an astounding coaching blunder kept the Irish from a perfect season. After demolishing eight straight opponents, including powerful Army, Minnesota, Georgia Tech, and the best Northwestern team in years, Notre Dame traveled to play Carnegie Tech.

The only doubt in anyone's mind was the size of the score the supremely confident Irish would run up. Rockne, blissfully unaware of the effect of what he was doing, decided to leave the team in the care of his assistants and attend the Army–Navy game in Chicago. The decision was also motivated by the fact that Rockne was writing a syndicated column and felt that he had to cover the game, which was the biggest attraction of the season. It matched Navy's best team ever against an Army club which had lost only once, by 7–0, to Notre Dame. The game, a wild, thrilling spectacle played before 110,000 at Soldier Field, ended in a 21–21 deadlock.

Rockne enjoyed it immensely and was in a jubilant mood when he asked the Western Union operator if any score had come in from Pittsburgh. It had, he was told. It was 19–0, a final. Rockne was happy for only a split second longer, until he heard that Notre Dame owned the zero.

Carnegie Tech, led by a furious defense, had simply outplayed Notre Dame from the first minute until the last. The Irish had given up only one touchdown in eight games, but they were pushed all over the field.

Judge Walter Steffen, Carnegie Tech's excellent coach and a former All-America quarterback under Stagg at Chicago twenty years before, had employed just the right psychology in elevating his team for the game. He played upon its injured pride at Rockne's absence and Notre Dame's condescension.

Ernie Nevers of Stanford. Pop
Warner thought that he was even better
than Thorpe. What more can anyone say?

It was not the first time that such a tactic was used to motivate an underdog, nor would it be the last. In the 1947 Rose Bowl game Illinois's coach, Ray Eliot, worked a similar technique to arouse a team which had been denigrated by the West Coast. The result was a rout of U.C.L.A. by the Illini. And Lou Little achieved perhaps the greatest Rose Bowl upset with his Columbia team, under comparable circumstances, in the 1934 game with Stanford.

Rockne, to his credit, reacted with the proper contrition, and his hold on the public's esteem was so great that he was probably the only coach in history who could have emerged from such a gaffe still employed. He was not even hanged in effigy at South Bend. A week later Rockne and the varsity made amends by winning from Howard Harding Jones's strong Southern California team 13–12.

This was the first meeting in what has since become the most exciting intersectional rivalry in football. Notre Dame won four out of five times while Rockne was coaching, three of the victories being by a single point. Southern California's unbeaten 1928 team won easily from Rockne's worst Irish eleven. But it was the 1930 game which Notre Dame fans never tire of reliving.

Rockne had struggled hopelessly with a subpar team in 1928. Its only moment of glory was the upset of Army, the game it won "for the Gipper." Rockne was also suffering from a serious illness diagnosed as phlebitis with complications. He was always an intense man, and now his nerves were being worn thin by extraordinary demands upon his time and energy. His troubles were not markedly different from those endured by many successful football coaches through the years. Those who lose come to know the peace and quiet of the unemployed. It is the smile of the bitch goddess that sets the angst level to rising.

In 1929 Notre Dame surprised the experts by sweeping through nine tough games unscathed. The schedule was now loaded with powerful opponents, such as Southern California, Army, Northwestern, Georgia Tech, and Carnegie Tech. The Irish traveled widely and were nicknamed the Nomads. Rockne's teams a decade earlier had wandered almost as freely and had been called the Ramblers. It was the best way to make Notre Dame a national byword, and it did not hurt any that nearly every trip ended with a victory party.

Notre Dame sent out a backfield on the perfect clubs of 1929 and 1930 that was even better than the Four Horsemen. It was bigger and faster at every position and gave away nothing on defense. The quartet of Frank Carideo at quarterback, Marchy Schwartz and Marty Brill at the halfbacks, and Jumping Joe Savoldi at fullback was quite possibly the finest in the school's history.

The 1930 Notre Dame team is believed to have been Rockne's best. This rating is based not so much upon its point totals as upon the caliber of the teams it defeated. It massacred a good Pennsylvania squad 60–20 to convince the Eastern writers of its ability. Powerful Pitt and Carnegie Tech were humbled, as were Southern Methodist and Navy. But it was in its last three games—in which it handed Northwestern and Army their only defeats and routed an excellent Southern California team—that Notre Dame showed how good it really was.

Northwestern, in particular, proved to be a seemingly immovable obstacle. The Wildcats, Big Ten co-champions, had their best team, led by Reb Russell and Pug Rentner. The line boasted superior tackles Dallas Marvil and John Riley, guard Wade Woodworth, and Frank Baker at end. These players were a worthy match for Notre Dame's forwards, who included Bert Metzger, Joe Kurth, Frank Hoffmann, and Tommy Yarr, some of the finest linemen the Irish have produced.

The contest took place at Dyche Stadium in Evanston before a sellout crowd of nearly 50,000. The winner would be a strong candidate for the mythical national championship. It was a furious defensive struggle, as expected, and for fifty-three minutes it was scoreless. Then, with electrifying suddenness, the brilliant Schwartz, later coach at Stanford, skipped through a momentary gap in the Purple line and ran 27 yards to a touchdown. Northwestern tried a desperation pass moments later, but Carideo intercepted to set up another touchdown, ensuring a 14–0 victory.

Now the Irish, worn out by what was to prove their toughest game, had to stagger against undefeated Army at Soldier Field, Chicago. The game was played in a driving sleet-and-rain storm with the field strongly resembling an ice rink. But once again Notre Dame's class told, and Army fell by the margin of an extra point, 7–6.

After defeating two such powerful elevens, Notre Dame had to travel across the country to face an awesome Southern California team which had beaten California 74–0, Stanford 41–12, U.C.L.A. 52–0, and Washington 32–0. The Trojans had scored 382 points with one of the most versatile and devastating offenses the West Coast—or anywhere else—had ever seen. Moreover, Rockne was lacking a fullback, since Savoldi had married and left school. But the Irish dipped into their able reserves and uncovered Bucky O'Connor. Then they went out and played probably the best game that any Rockne team had ever played. The score was 27–0, and Notre Dame had proved itself one of the great teams in history. To have won any of its last three games would have been a considerable accomplishment. To have won them all, and especially to have so completely routed the superb Trojans, was little short of miraculous.

Rockne's best team was, as football was to learn to its sorrow, also his last one. Before another season came he died in a plane crash in Kansas, mourned by millions—in sophisticated cities and in rustic villages, even as small and far away as his native Voss, Norway.

In thirteen years under the Golden Dome he saw his teams triumph 105 times and lose only 12, the finest winning percentage in the history of coaching. His impact upon Notre Dame, moreover, and upon the sport itself, has been so profound that more than four decades after his death he still remains the giant of his profession, and his alma mater a synonym for the game of football.

11. The Iceman Cometh

Nobody seemed quite able to describe the elusive halfback who began his varsity career at Champaign in October of 1923. The sportswriters were torn, strangely, between references to fire, ice, superman, and the supernatural. "A streak of fire, a breath of flame," wrote Grantland Rice. "The Wheaton Iceman," said another. "He is three or four men and a horse rolled into one," said Damon Runyon. Zuppke never did learn to pronounce his last name correctly. "Grainch," he kept calling him. But the appellation did not matter. Every football fan would soon know perfectly well who the halfback was, and his number too. It was 77, and he was the Galloping Ghost—Red Grange of Illinois.

There had been great runners before and there would be great ones after: Berwanger, Harmon, Davis, and O. J. Simpson. But there never was a ballcarrier who so captured the attention of the nation. Red Grange personified football in the Roaring Twenties the way Babe Ruth personified baseball, Bill Tilden tennis, Bobby Jones golf, and Jack Dempsey boxing.

Grange filled the grandstands wherever he appeared. Illinois dedicated its Memorial Stadium one afternoon in his junior year, when it played Michigan, and all the Iceman did was score four touchdowns in the first twelve minutes— the most incredible individual effort in history. He was nearly as good a year later at Franklin Field against Pennsylvania, where he ran for 363 yards on a muddy field. The East had

come to see, and stayed to gape. This was indeed three or four men and a horse all in one.

It was in his sophomore year that Grange had his strongest supporting cast, as Illinois rolled through eight games without defeat or tie and claimed the mythical national championship. He had two of the finest blockers any runner could have wished for in Earl Britton and Wally McIlwain. Britton would spring Grange at the line of scrimmage, and McIlwain would cut down potential tacklers in the open field. Zuppke said that McIlwain was the finest downfield blocker of all time, and Grange himself was always generous in praise of the two who cleared his path.

No one ever determined exactly what it was that made Grange so difficult to stop. It was not his size, for he weighed only 170 pounds. He was extremely fast, but there were others just as swift. He had a good change of pace and a dazzling cutback, but more than one of his contemporaries could match both maneuvers. What may have set him apart, however, was a sixth sense, combined with unusually acute peripheral vision. He seemed to know just when a tackler was approaching and exactly how to evade his grasp.

It must not be supposed, however, that no team ever stopped Grange. Minnesota shackled him in 1924 by completely outplaying the Illinois line, and Nebraska, Iowa, Michigan, and Chicago held him in check the next year.

By the time Grange was a senior, injuries to the team's quarterbacks forced him into the signal-calling role. He did a more than creditable job, but he was really a natural halfback, and his passing, although accurate, was not a major threat.

The two games upon which Grange's fame rests are the Michigan encounter of 1924 and the Pennsylvania affair one year later. Against the Wolverines, unbeaten in the two previous seasons, Grange ran the opening kickoff 95 yards to a touchdown, then scored on runs of 67, 56, and 45 yards within the next twelve minutes.

Michigan was coached by George Little that year, and not by Fielding Yost, who had been ordered by his doctors to take a rest. But it would have made no difference if Yost had been directing Michigan. Grange and the Illini were playing like

Red Grange, the Galloping Ghost of Illinois. "All Grange can do is run," scoffed The Michigan Daily *before the 1924 game. "Yes," answered Zuppke, "and all Galli-Curci can do is sing."*

97

men possessed. They could do nothing wrong, and the 39–14 score was the biggest of the century, until then, against a Michigan team. In fact, only five times since has an opponent scored more points against the Maize and Blue.

Grange carried the ball fifteen times from scrimmage for 212 yards and four touchdowns, completed six of eight passes for 64 yards and another score, and ran three kickoffs back for 126 yards, one of them all the way. His efforts for the day resulted in a gain of 402 yards. He scored five touchdowns himself and passed for one.

At Franklin Field the next year, against an undefeated Pennsylvania team, Grange carried the ball twenty-eight times for 237 yards, caught a pair of passes for 35 more, ran two punts back for 12, and two kickoffs for 79. He scored three times as Illinois ruined the Quakers 24–2.

The accomplishments against Pennsylvania, although not as spectacular as the ones in the Michigan game, may have been even more remarkable. Grange had a weaker team in front of him in 1925, and the field at Philadelphia was deep in mud.

Except for the Penn triumph, Grange's final year was one of frustration. The game which might have lifted the gloom was the return engagement with arch rival Michigan.

Fielding Yost had overruled his doctors and come back for two more seasons as head coach. He had, in 1925, the team he was to call the best ever at Ann Arbor, better even than his celebrated point-a-minute machines of 1901–05.

The Wolverines had their traditionally stingy defense, even more unyielding than usual, and they had developed a scoring capability that awed their opponents. In passer Benny Friedman and receiver Bennie Oosterbaan, Michigan came up with the most famous aerial combination up to that time and one of the best in football history.

Benny-to-Bennie delighted onlookers all over the Midwest with their electrifying touchdown plays. Friedman was a brilliant strategist, a dangerous runner, and an expert field-goal kicker, as well as an alert pass defender. Oosterbaan was an uncanny receiver with a knack of filtering through an opposing secondary and making sure-handed catches. His defensive ability marked him as one of the two or three best of all time,

98

Michigan men. Coach Fielding H. "Hurry-up" Yost brings Benny Friedman (left) and Bennie Oosterbaan to the White House in 1926 to meet President Calvin Coolidge.

and there are still many students of the game who rate Oosterbaan as the greatest end who ever played in college.

To go with these superstars Yost had an array of agile, opportunistic linemen and a bevy of versatile backs. No member of the team weighed over 200 pounds, but they more than made up for lack of heft with their unexcelled ability to play as a coordinated unit.

In eight games this team scored 227 points to 3 for all opponents. In the forty-eight years since, no Big Ten team has equaled Michigan's defensive record. It also had the distinction of handing Navy its worst defeat in history, 54–0. But it was in the game against Illinois that the defense really came into its own.

In the same stadium where it had been humiliated a year earlier, Michigan, bolstered by some brilliant sophomores, outplayed the Illinois line and held Grange to 64 yards in twenty-one trips with the ball. In the 1924 game he had made more than that on the opening kickoff. A heavy rain helped to slow Grange down, but it also put an end to Friedman's passing. He managed to place-kick a field goal, however, and that was all the scoring, as the Wolverines won 3–0. Oosterbaan, though only a sophomore, played an inspired game, continually forcing Grange to run inside tackle, where he was smothered.

There was no doubt in any Midwesterner's mind that Michigan was the top team of 1925, and perhaps the best in a generation. But, incredibly, it lost a game. The defeat came at the hands of a sturdy Northwestern club, with a monumental assist from the Chicago weatherman. For five days preceding the game it rained in torrents. Soldier Field became a vast puddle, with the mud engulfing the players almost like quicksand. Nearly everyone thought that the Wildcats would have been slaughtered on a dry field and that they would still lose—although in a low-scoring game—in the mud. It turned out, however, that no passing was possible, which neutralized Friedman and Oosterbaan. Rushing was also futile, unless the ballcarrier had lettered in swimming. Michigan gained a total of 35 yards, Northwestern 28. The Purple picked up a fumble early in the game, kicked a field goal, and held on thereafter. An intentional safety was given to allow better field position for a punt, thereby frustrating any Michigan hopes of blocking it and scoring a touchdown.

Thus Michigan lost what Big Ten fans referred to as "the baseball game" by a score of 3–2 and saw Dartmouth and Alabama claim the mythical national championship. Yost's enthusiasm for his team remained undiminished, however. He thought that the defeat had been largely at the hands of the weatherman and that the 10–0 victory over a good Ohio State team and the 35–0 rout of powerful Minnesota on the next two Saturdays were more indicative of Michigan's ability.

Yost had decided to stay for one more year as coach before stepping up to the position of athletic director. He could not retire while Friedman was still around to throw passes to Oosterbaan. Many of their supporting cast had graduated, however, and the victories were not nearly so lopsided as before. But, still, they came, except for a 10–0 loss to Navy's undefeated team. In the Big Ten, the Wolverines were atop the standings when they went to play Ohio State in the next-to-last game of 1926.

Columbus was jammed with half-crazed Buckeye fans who had come to see their unbeaten heroes dispose of Michigan and win the Big Ten title. Ticket managers at Ohio Stadium realized to their dismay that thousands were massing to storm the gates. In a desperate effort to placate the mob, standing room was allowed, and all of the statutes governing overcrowding were ignored. When over 90,000 had squeezed into the horseshoe and there were still more people pushing against the gates, a riot broke out in which a number of fans were hurt. Those who had managed to get in, however, saw perhaps the wildest game in what has been a series replete with them.

Ohio State moved out to a 10–0 lead and appeared to have Michigan on the run when Friedman began to find Oosterbaan with short, accurate passes. The Wolverines trailed by only 3 points and were on the Buckeye 44-yard line with a few seconds remaining in the half. Despite the distance and a difficult angle, Friedman elected to try a field goal. As the holder, Lou Gilbert, knelt, Oosterbaan ran over, whispered something to him, then ran back to his end position. Ohio State, certain that a trick pass play was coming, concentrated on covering Oosterbaan and delayed its rush, thereby giving Friedman time to kick an astonishing field goal.

In the second half the Michigan passing combination clicked again, and the game drew to a close with the visitors clinging to a 17–10 advantage. Fighting to the very end, however, the Buckeyes moved inexorably down the field on the running of their fullback, Marty Karow. With seconds remaining, he crossed the goal line. Now only a point separated Ohio State from a tie. Myers Clark, who had kicked a field goal, was chosen to convert. But as darkness and hysteria descended upon the stadium, his effort went awry under a frenzied rush from the Michigan line.

A week later, the exhausted Wolverines traveled to Minnesota for Yost's last game as head coach. The Gophers, big

101

Benny Friedman of Michigan has just thrown one of his celebrated passes, no doubt to Bennie Oosterbaan somewhere out of camera range. And most probably out of range of the defense as well.

and angry, were tired of losing to Michigan after seven straight setbacks. They pushed the smaller visitors up and down the field, piling up more than 300 yards on the ground and taking a 6–0 lead. But whenever Minnesota seemed on the verge of adding another touchdown and breaking the game open, either the alert Friedman would intercept a pass or the desperate Michigan line would summon its last ounce of strength and take possession.

As the second half wore on, the freezing cold ended any passing threat Michigan might have hoped would get it on the scoreboard. The frozen field did not slow the Gophers' running game, however, and with fullback Herb Joesting bolting for huge gains, it seemed only a matter of time before another score would be made.

Joesting, All-America fullback, was nicknamed the Hammer of Thor because of his pulverizing rushes. As a line plunger he was considered comparable even to the great Nevers of Stanford.

Michigan appeared finished when Minnesota's halfback Mally Nydahl swung into the open and started downfield, but he fumbled when tackled, and the ball was scooped up on the dead run by Oosterbaan. While 60,000 crestfallen fans groaned in despair, the Michigan star ran 60 yards for a touchdown to tie the score. Friedman then added the extra point, and Michigan celebrated another Big Ten championship.

It was the end of Yost's unparalleled career. In twenty-five seasons his Wolverines had won 165 times and lost only 29. The final victory, against a vastly superior team which had dominated play in all except the most crucial situations, proved again the Yostian theory that games were most often decided by mistakes. He had drilled his ends to scoop up a fumble and run with it, in the hope that cold weather and hard tackling might present such an opportunity.

Yost contended that good teams made their own luck— and also that good coaches ought to know when to retire. After proudly congratulating his immortal passing duo on their final game together, he sat back, lighted a big cigar, and contradicted his celebrated nickname. Hurry-Up Yost, at long last, had finally slowed down.

103

12. Wrong-Way Riegels

Football had been played on the Pacific Coast for more than thirty years before the rest of the country would acknowledge a Western team as national champion.

Three men, all from the East, raised the caliber of the game on the Coast. Andy Smith, a former fullback and later coach at Pennsylvania and Purdue, went to the University of California at Berkeley. Howard Harding Jones, onetime Yale player and coach at New Haven and Iowa City, took over at Southern California. And Pop Warner moved from Pittsburgh to Stanford. These men flourished in the twenties, as the rise of West Coast football coincided with the return of the Rose Bowl game.

The Pasadena officials, having tired of chariot racing as their New Year's Day attraction, had decided in 1916 to give football another try. This time, however, they were careful to invite weak teams from the East. Brown and Pennsylvania came out in 1916 and 1917 and were disposed of with alacrity by Washington State and Oregon respectively. But the games were dull, with the only excitement being provided by the presence of William H. "Lone Star" Dietz, coach of Washington State.

Dietz had been a teammate of Jim Thorpe's at Carlisle and later served as Pop Warner's assistant. He was a superb coach, but football occupied only a small portion of his complex and creative mind. He was well-read, had a flair for the theater, music, and the arts, and was a raconteur of such splendid gifts that fellow coaches sat spellbound at his feet.

The Tournament fathers realized quickly that if they wanted to save the Rose Bowl, they would have to invite the best Eastern team and hope that it did not humiliate the West Coast champion.

Harvard, the country's strongest eleven in 1919, accepted a bid and was expected to take Oregon in stride. The Ducks from Eugene, however, played far above their season's form and held the Crimson to a 7–6 score. It was such a good showing that respect for Pacific Coast football rose rapidly in the East. But in the Big Ten skepticism still remained.

Andy Smith and the Golden Bears of the University of California changed that, however, in one short afternoon at Pasadena. The date was January 1, 1921, and from then on, West Coast football has been the equal of that played anywhere.

Smith's 1920 California team was so good that it obliterated eight opponents, rolling up 482 points and allowing only 14. It won the accolade the "Wonder Team." California had perfect seasons in 1921 and 1922 and undefeated but tied teams in 1923 and 1924. In all, the Golden Bears went through fifty games without defeat, a record never matched on the Coast in the years since. The five unbeaten squads all shared in the nickname Wonder Teams, but the 1920 club was probably the strongest.

It had the Coast's first superstar in Harold "Brick" Muller, All-America end. Muller was a devastating blocker, expert pass catcher, and flawless defensive player, with the size, at 215 pounds, to stop off-tackle runs by an opponent. In addition, he could throw the ball farther than any California backfield man. The Bears had a well-coordinated offense, with Boots Erb at quarterback, Pesky Sprott and Crip Toomey at the halfbacks, and Archie Nisbet at fullback. Their line was big and mobile, and their confidence was unbounded.

Ohio State's undefeated and untied Big Ten champions were chosen as California's Rose Bowl opponent. The Buckeyes could not match their host in statistics, but the experts felt that the caliber of their Big Ten opposition was far superior to that of the teams California had beaten. Most observers foresaw an Ohio State victory in a close game.

They were wrong. The Buckeyes never even scored. California whipped the Big Ten's best team 28–0, and Columbus went into deep mourning. The experts had trouble believing the result as much for its margin as for the apparent ease with which the Bears toyed with their victims.

What had been overlooked was the fact that Ohio State was a smaller team with a definite weakness on pass defense. California's heavier line opened holes for its runners, and Brick Muller threw a 53-yard touchdown pass that broke the Buckeyes' spirit. This was the celebrated Muller-to-Stephens pass, the length of which was a lively topic of discussion for years in every place but Columbus, where it was charitably not brought up. California had worked out the play to take advantage of Muller's phenomenal throwing ability. He received a lateral from Sprott and circled deep in the backfield while Stephens raced far down the field past the Ohio State halfbacks. No one outside of the California varsity thought a football could be thrown that far, but Muller wound up and lined a bullet pass the whole distance.

The Buckeyes had been shaken in the early moments of the game when they had been thrown back twice, after long marches, near the goal line. California had then scored to further discomfort the Midwesterners. Now Muller knocked the last hopes from under them, and only the size of the final humiliation was in doubt.

Some Ohio State players felt that the 85-degree temperatures had sapped their energy, but they undoubtedly would have lost anywhere under any conditions. They had been outrushed 234 yards to 85.

The Buckeyes were a good team, which had been resourceful and had won several games in the last minute. But in California they were up against one of the great teams in Rose Bowl history.

The repercussions of the California victory echoed from coast to coast. Even a scoreless tie in Pasadena a year later with Washington and Jefferson did not lower respect for the Bears, since the game had been played in the mud and the Presidents were acknowledged to have an excellent team themselves, led by the versatile tackle Russ Stein.

106

By the time the "Big Game" of 1924 was at hand, everyone was wondering when California would finally lose. The partisans of Stanford had high hopes that their team, coached for the first time by Pop Warner, could supply the answer. But the Indians received a seemingly mortal blow when Ernie Nevers fractured his ankle.

With their greatest player on the bench, Stanford hung on grimly into the waning moments of the fourth quarter, trailing the Bears by 20–6. It appeared certain, with only four minutes left, that California would win and advance to the Rose Bowl to meet the Four Horsemen.

But little Murray Cuddeback of Stanford went on a rampage, throwing and catching passes with unerring skill. Stanford scored to narrow the gap to a touchdown, and as the final gun sounded, he dashed across the goal line with a touchdown pass that now made the score 20–19. Then Cuddeback kicked a perfect extra point to earn Stanford a tie in what has ever after been remembered as the most exciting game between the two schools.

Walter Camp had come to see the festivities, having been told that the California–Stanford "Big Game" was the West Coast version of Harvard versus Yale. Camp was not disappointed and afterward said it had been the most thrilling finish he had ever seen.

Stanford kept the Pasadena engagement with Notre Dame. California booked a postseason date in Berkeley with the undefeated Pennsylvania team, which was rated the East's strongest. The Golden Bears won a hard-fought game, 14–0, to further increase the stature of Coast football.

When California finally did lose to another college, in 1925, it took one of the best Washington teams ever, led by All-America halfback George Wilson, to accomplish the feat.

Stanford and Southern California fought for supremacy in the West after California slipped from the top. In 1925 Howard Harding Jones arrived on the Southern California campus, and for the next sixteen years the Trojans were in the thick of nearly every scramble for the Rose Bowl.

Jones had worked miracles at Iowa, where he gave the Hawkeyes two perfect seasons in succession in 1921 and 1922.

Iowa had never seen anything like the 1921 club, with all eleven starters being from within the state and each an excellent performer.

The standout in the line was Fred "Duke" Slater, a big, fast, courageous tackle whose spirit inspired his colleagues. Slater, an All-America, rates as one of the best at his position ever to play in the Big Ten.

In the backfield Iowa had "Devine" guidance. At quarterback was Aubrey Devine. At the halfbacks were his brother Glenn Devine and Craven Shuttleworth. Gordon Locke played fullback. This quartet gave away nothing in ability to the Four Horsemen. What it lacked was a Grantland Rice to rhapsodize over its accomplishments. In the Jones system of offense the quarterback, Aubrey Devine, and fullback, Locke, did nearly all of the ball handling. Aubrey Devine was a marvelous runner and passer who played supremely well under pressure. Locke possessed unusual speed for a line plunger. Both were All-America choices.

The Hawkeyes played their big game against Notre Dame that year and won it 10–7. It was Rockne's only loss, and spoiled what would have been a third consecutive perfect season.

Iowa rolled through the Big Ten, then repeated the performance the next year, although sharing the title with Michigan. In 1922 Jones took his club to New Haven to play his brother Tad's strong Yale eleven. It was one of the best games of the season, with Iowa emerging a 6–0 winner.

Howard Jones, who bore the nickname the Head Man, was an introverted, painstaking analyst of the game, not given to the easy familiarity of a Rockne or a Zuppke. At Southern Cal he instituted the same offense which had worked at Iowa, and through the years the Trojans became known for an explosive mixture of passing, power running, and blocking.

The roster of All-America backs coached by Jones reads like a who's who of the best on the Coast during the late twenties and early thirties. Mort Kaer, Morley Drury, Erny Pinckert, Gus Shaver, and Cotton Warburton would all have been strong Heisman Trophy contenders had there been such an award then.

Pinckert may well have been the best blocking back the West ever produced. He rates in a class with Earl Britton and Wally McIlwain, who blocked for Grange at Illinois, and Forest Evashevski, interferer extraordinary for the great Tom Harmon at Michigan. Drury rushed for more than a thousand yards at a time when such a feat was almost miraculous.

But all of these good backfield men could have gone nowhere without the powerful Trojan forwards to clear their paths and contain opponents as well. Here Jones turned out top players of the caliber of Jesse Hibbs, John Baker, and Aaron Rosenberg.

This wealth of talent gave Southern Cal three Rose Bowl victories—all over undefeated teams—three national championships, and four West Coast titles. When anybody did beat the Trojans between 1925 and 1933, and it was rare, the margin was usually miniscule. Eighty-four games were won and only eleven lost, five by a single point (three to Notre Dame and Rockne).

The lone occasion on which U.S.C. was outclassed was in the 1930 game with Rockne's last and best Notre Dame team. The 27–0 defeat was the worst Jones suffered in sixteen years at Southern Cal. No other opponent ever registered that many points against his defenses.

It was after the 1929 season that Howard Jones first took Southern California to the Rose Bowl. He had passed up the game the year before, even though the Trojans were the best team in the West (and the nation as well), because the university was having a feud with the game's sponsors.

The opponent was Jock Sutherland's undefeated, untied Pittsburgh powerhouse, led by its smooth-running All-America tailback, Octavius "Toby" Uansa, and the best end in the country, Joe Donchess.

Even though the Trojans had scored 445 points to only 52 for eleven opponents, they had still managed to lose two games: one to Notre Dame by a point, and the other to California by a touchdown. In both defeats Southern Cal had not been able to pass well when its running game was contained.

Pitt was determined to stop the Trojans on the ground, and did a reasonably good job. But with four passes in the first half, Russ Saunders and his receivers succeeded in destroying the Panthers. All Saunders did was throw the ball to the open man, which was easy, since Pitt's secondary was constantly out of position closing in to stop running plays.

It was 26–0 at halftime, and Sutherland was already sorry he had made the trip. The final score was 47–14, one of the worst defeats any team has ever suffered in the Rose Bowl. Eastern writers were more surprised than they should have been, since a glance at Southern Cal's final regular-season game would have revealed a 45–13 rout of Carnegie Tech, a big-time football power then.

It seemed inconceivable to the chagrined Pittsburgh followers that their team could be so humiliated, and they were certain that if they ever came back, history could not repeat itself.

They were wrong. In 1932 Pitt went unbeaten again, although tied twice, and returned to Pasadena. This time Southern Cal had a perfect record and a flawless defensive club, but not much of a scoring potential. The experts anticipated a low point total.

They too were wrong. The Trojans won 35–0, burying Pitt with three last-quarter touchdowns. This time it was not passing, but simply a matter of a bigger line smothering a smaller line and of Cotton Warburton and Homer Griffith dancing away from the Pitt tacklers.

The year before, Jones had put what may have been his best team into the Rose Bowl. The 1931 Trojans, nicknamed the Thundering Herd, were victimized by St. Mary's in their opener, then proceeded to destroy every opponent on a difficult schedule. The high point of their season came in November at South Bend, although for three periods it appeared to be just the opposite. Rockne was gone, but his assistants had turned out another awesome team, and it led 14–0 going into the last quarter.

Here the embattled Trojans rallied to earn one of the truly memorable triumphs, not only in their own rich history but in the annals of football as well. With heroic passing from Gus Shaver, Southern Cal narrowed the gap to 14–13 and

110

seemed on the verge of losing still another game by 1 point to Notre Dame. But John Baker, the All-America guard, kicked a field goal in the final minutes for a 16–14 victory. Notre Dame's undefeated streak was thus broken at twenty-six games.

The Trojans coasted into the 1932 Rose Bowl against Tulane confident that they could now defeat any team. The Green Wave, coached by Bernie Bierman and led by All-America end Jerry Dalrymple and halfback Don Zimmerman, was claiming the national championship on the basis of eleven straight victories and a point total of 338 to 35. It was the best team in Tulane's history and Bierman's last before leaving for Minnesota.

Southern Cal's statistics were remarkably similar, with 342 points having been scored against only 40. The one contrasting note was in the two teams' performances against a common foe, Georgia. Tulane had won by two touchdowns, while the Trojans had humiliated the Georgians 60–0, their worst loss ever.

In the Rose Bowl the Southern Cal running game demonstrated its power early, with Pinckert fooling Tulane by becoming a ballcarrier. The Green Wave knew that he would have to be contained as a blocker if it was to have any hope of stopping Southern Cal. Shaver knew this too and slipped the ball twice to Pinckert in crucial situations. Both times the peerless blocker bolted through the Green Wave's defenses, letting others do the interfering for a change. His dashes for touchdowns helped the host team to build up a 21–0 lead. Tulane fought back grimly and outplayed Southern Cal for most of the game, but could score only 12 points.

The Trojans gained wide recognition during these Rose Bowl years, but it is also possible that the teams of 1926-27-28, none of which played at Pasadena, were just as formidable. These clubs, led by Drury and Kaer, met a total of three defeats, all by one point. The losses in 1926 were to Stanford and Notre Dame by identical 13–12 scores. The next year the spoiler was Notre Dame again, 7–6. In 1928 the Trojans achieved an undefeated season, although tied by California.

The Bears were invited to Pasadena, and thus their center got his chance to become a football immortal. Yet it is understandable that, but for the honor of it all, he might just as well have preferred to remain a face in the crowd. His name was Roy Riegels.

When Stumpy Thomason of Georgia Tech fumbled, Riegels clutched the ball and started for the Engineers' goal. Somehow, in avoiding two onrushing tacklers, he became disoriented and changed direction, galloping toward the opposite end of the field. His teammate Benny Lom chased him for 60 yards, but the screams of the crowd obliterated his entreaties. When Lom finally overtook his misguided colleague, they were a yard from their own goal. A wave of Tech men engulfed them, and only then did it dawn upon California's center that he had become a legend: Wrong-Way Riegels. The Bears still had possession of the ball, but not of their composure, and no one could blame them. Lom tried to punt out of danger. The kick was blocked, however, giving Georgia Tech a safety.

Riegels played the entire second half and saw his team lose by a score of 8–7. It took exceptional courage to stay in the game, as well as to come back the next year, and Riegels' teammates showed their respect by electing him captain. He played well in 1929, but the Bears did not get the chance to return to Pasadena.

Riegels was neither the first nor the last player to go the wrong way. In football's inaugural, some happily anonymous Rutgers man had become confused and kicked the ball toward his own goal, enabling Princeton to score.

Riegels performed his feat, however, in the most publicized game of the year. If he had committed the gaffe in some early-season scrimmage with the Santa Barbara Teachers, it would have been of only minor concern. But in the Rose Bowl it dominated every front page, and in spite of some almost equally bizarre happenings since, the incredible run of Wrong-Way Riegels remains the most famous single play in the history of football.

The most famous play in football,
Roy Riegels' wrong-way run in the 1929
Rose Bowl game. Riegels wears number 11.

13. The Edison of the Gridiron

All New York was waiting that November afternoon in 1928 to see Pop Warner's new invention. The Edison of the gridiron had come to the big town with his mighty Stanford Indians to show the Army and the East his new double wingback formation.

The experts wondered why the single wingback formation was not still good enough for the man who had devised it too. Warner explained that by placing a halfback outside each end, he opened the way for a whole new series of double reverses, improved the pass-receiving possibilities, and gave equal blocking power to wide plays around either side. It all sounded a bit visionary to the reactionaries, but after everyone watched a good Army team run around in circles trying to find the ball, it was apparent that Glenn Scobey Warner had indeed turned the gridiron upside down again.

Stanford ran around and through the Army and flung the ball to miraculously uncovered receivers for a 26–0 victory that astounded everyone. Some tried to downgrade Army, but the Cadets had won eight out of nine games, losing only to Notre Dame by a touchdown in the one the Irish won "for the Gipper." Army had done about as well as any team could have under such circumstances.

Soon the double wingback formation was showing up in the repertoire of every big-time eleven. Andy Kerr, Warner's most devoted assistant, was to have remarkable success with it at Colgate, creating in 1932 a team that went undefeated, untied, and unscored upon. And when Kerr and the Red

115

Raiders were overlooked by the Rose Bowl, the word "uninvited" was added.

All Warner needed to make his double wing work to perfection—in addition to good linemen, of course—was a fullback who could run with power, sweep the ends, and throw accurate passes. The incomparable Ernie Nevers met these specifications perfectly, as did the excellent Biff Hoffman.

Stanford enjoyed a perfect season in 1926, went to the Rose Bowl, and completely outplayed Alabama. A blocked punt late in the game, however, gave the Southern champions a chance for a tie. They got it, and Stanford had to be content with a statistical victory only. Nevertheless, most experts rated the Indians and Navy as the two best teams of the season.

The following year Warner again took his team to Pasadena, this time to engage Pittsburgh, his former employer. The Pitt team was directed by Jock Sutherland, a fine tackle on Warner's invincible Panther elevens before the war. Stanford won a tense 7–6 decision, as both touchdowns revolved around Frankie Wilton of the Indians. His fumble gave Pitt its touchdown, but he redeemed himself later when he scooped up a teammate's fumble and ran it over the goal to tie the score. Hoffman then kicked the extra point to give Pop Warner his only Rose Bowl victory.

Stanford never did make it back to Pasadena while Warner was its coach. Southern California began its domination of West Coast football, and the best the Indians could do for a while was to finish second. They had excellent personnel, an inexhaustible supply of plays, and one of the greatest coaches in the game.

But Southern Cal had practically the same assets, and its roster was even deeper in talented players. A tie and five straight defeats at Southern Cal's hands finally drove Warner out of Palo Alto. The games were usually close, with the exception of the Trojans' 41–12 landslide in 1930. But close was not what Stanford men wanted.

The rage to beat Southern Cal reached its peak with the freshman players who came to Palo Alto in 1932. They lost to the Trojan freshmen, and then took an oath never again to lose to U.S.C., thus becoming known as the Vow Boys.

Freshman resolutions being what they are, few people took the Vow Boys seriously, least of all Southern California, which expected to have another powerhouse in 1933. The Trojans had Warburton in the backfield and Rosenberg in the line, and there were not two better players in the country. But these cheeky Stanford freshmen were no ordinary football players themselves. Included among them were some of Stanford's all-time stars. Monk Moscrip at end, Bob Reynolds at tackle, Frank Alustiza at quarterback, Bones Hamilton at halfback, and Bobby Grayson at fullback would, before their careers ended, be acknowledged the best in the country at their respective positions.

Tiny Thornhill, another of Pop Warner's former Pittsburgh linemen, had become head coach at Palo Alto in 1933, and he fell heir to this talent bonanza. The double wing offense still required a multipurpose fullback, and Grayson was just what Thornhill needed.

Stanford and Southern California headed for their showdown with a Rose Bowl bid riding on the outcome. It was the kind of game everyone had expected, with each side earning one touchdown, but Stanford also scored a pair of field goals for a 13–7 victory that set off dancing in the streets of Palo Alto. It was the first defeat in a twenty-seven-game span for Southern California, and it marked the beginning of a five-year recession in Trojan football. Not until 1938 would Howard Jones field another nationally ranked team.

The Vow Boys not only had broken the U.S.C. jinx but also had set Stanford on a course for Pasadena. They were to whip Southern Cal twice more, to fulfill their oath, but in the Rose Bowl they had their troubles. First it was Columbia and then it was Alabama. Losing to Columbia was a surprise, but nearly everybody in those years was losing to Alabama.

The Crimson Tide from Tuscaloosa first sent a team to the Rose Bowl at the end of the 1925 season. This was the perfect-record club led by Johnny Mack Brown and Pooley Hubert. It was strong on defense, good at running wide, and capable of accurate passing to score quickly. This is just what it did in defeating Washington in the Rose Bowl, as Brown dazzled the Huskies with open-field running and Hubert showed a devastating passing skill. Alabama scored three touchdowns in seven minutes of the third period to wipe out a big Washington lead.

All of the good work done by Washington's All-America titan, George Wilson, was nullified by the Alabama explosion. Wilson was the key to everything the Huskies did on both offense and defense. Washington backers noted that he had been injured all the time Alabama was making its touchdowns, and that while he was in action the Huskies had a 19–0 margin. But Alabama's partisans simply pointed to the final score of 20–19, content that even though Wilson was the finest performer on the field, they had the better team.

Southern football had produced a number of first-rate elevens long before Alabama's victory in the Rose Bowl, but somehow the section had seldom been able to convince the rest of the country of this fact. The only notable exceptions were Georgia Tech's widely acknowledged champions in 1917 and several Vanderbilt clubs of earlier years, which had impressed the East and Midwest by their strong play against Harvard, Yale, and Michigan.

Wallace Wade, who had been a guard on Brown University's Rose Bowl team in 1916, was the coach responsible for bringing big-time football to Tuscaloosa.

Another graduate of an Eastern institution, Robert R. Neyland of West Point, became head coach at Tennessee a few years later. Immediately, Alabama and Tennessee moved to the front among the Dixie teams.

Bernie Bierman, the old Minnesota star, had moved in at Tulane, replacing another former Gopher, Clark Shaughnessy. And William A. Alexander had taken over from Heisman at Georgia Tech. Both Tech and Tulane had their good teams, even some great ones, such as the Engineers of 1928 and the Green Wave elevens of 1929 and 1931.

But for consistent powerhouses, nobody could match Alabama and Tennessee. Their annual game soon turned into the biggest football attraction in the South. Tennessee's coming of age, in fact, dates from the 1928 game against Alabama, in which Gene McEver returned the opening kickoff for a touchdown and the Volunteers went on to a monumental 15–13 victory.

McEver, the "Mack" of Tennessee's celebrated "Hack and Mack" touchdown twins (Buddy Hackman was the other), rates as perhaps the greatest in a long line of standout backfield stars developed by Neyland.

Tennessee's 1928 team was loaded with new players— the Flaming Sophomores—who bore an amazing resemblance to Stanford's Vow Boys in that they performed in their very first season with the skill and poise of much more experienced players.

Their coach quickly became the master defensive strategist of the South—and of the nation as well. Neyland had been a brilliant engineer at West Point and had continued his studies at M.I.T. He approached the problems of the defensive game with the cool detachment of an engineer laying out plans for a highway. He was a stern disciplinarian, and his players soon learned that with the General, football was identical to a problem in military tactics.

Neyland, like Fielding Yost, won his games on the other side's mistakes. His offense was simple and basic, with the power single wing thrusts of such famed runners as Beattie Feathers and George "Bad News" Cafego preceded by devastating blocking. There were only a few plays, but they were executed with perfect efficiency.

But occasionally, when he had a strategist and ball handler of the caliber of Bobby Dodd, Neyland's offense showed a touch of razzle-dazzle. Dodd, when he later became coach at Georgia Tech, gained national attention for his bewildering offensive intricacies. Neyland, however, was more a creature of the old school, and his best teams usually ran over rather than around their opponents.

With his devotion to fundamentals and line play, it was not surprising that Neyland developed some of the game's best forwards. Especially at guard, Tennessee seemed to have a bottomless reservoir of talent. Herman Hickman (later coach at Yale), Bob Suffridge, and Ed Molinski were All-

119

America choices, with Hickman and Suffridge being mentioned on many all-time teams as well.

Neyland coached at Knoxville for twenty-one years, during which time his squads won 173 and lost only 31. Nine of his teams were undefeated. In his first seven years, Tennessee won 61 and lost only 2.

Later in the thirties the Vols turned out three perfect-record teams in succession in regular-season play, including one that held all opponents scoreless—the last major college to accomplish this feat. Against arch rival Alabama, Neyland saw his teams win twelve times, tie twice, and drop only five games. Critics sometimes denigrated Tennessee's winning percentage in Neyland's early years by charging that the Vols never played any of the strong teams from the East, Midwest, or Pacific Coast.

In contrast, Alabama went to six Rose Bowls, winning four, losing one, and tying one. It was one of those Crimson Tide Rose Bowl teams that handed the Flaming Sophomores their only defeat in three years of varsity play.

The 1930 Alabama club, led by two All-America nominees, tackle Fred Sington and fullback Jim "Sugar" Cain, was a typical Wallace Wade team of fast, clever, and hard-tackling oportunists. It yielded only two touchdowns all season.

This may well have been the best of Wade's three Rose Bowl teams, although it lacked the flamboyance of Johnny Mack Brown's 1925 eleven. It marched over Tennessee by an 18–6 score, leaving no doubt that it was the South's best team. Then Washington State, with Mel Hein and Turk Edwards in its line, was crushed in the Rose Bowl. Alabama had enough sense not to match weight with the big Cougars. Instead, its speed and deception combined with an aerial assault to befuddle Washington State's defense.

Wade moved to Duke after the season, but Alabama's fortunes did not suffer. His replacement was Frank Thomas, one of Rockne's most astute quarterbacks at Notre Dame during the Gipp years. Thomas coached for fifteen seasons at Tuscaloosa, giving the Crimson Tide some of its greatest teams and compiling a record of 115 victories against only

24 defeats. He had a difficult time with Neyland, however, winning 3, but losing 6, with 1 tie.

Thomas turned out some of Alabama's finest players, with the pass-catching wizard Don Hutson being undoubtedly the most renowned. His partner, Dixie Howell, and quarterback Riley Smith, were also stars of a memorable 1934 team. The deadly accurate jump passer Harry Gilmer led another unbeaten Rose Bowl champion a decade later.

The Alabama team that played against Stanford's Vow Boys on New Year's Day 1935 made a profound impression upon football coaches. It destroyed a powerful Stanford defense with the deft aerials of Howell and the amazing catches of Hutson and the other end, Paul "Bear" Bryant.

The passing game had been catching on, especially in the Southwest Conference, where Southern Methodist was being called the Aerial Circus. But many coaches still clung to the idea that there was too much risk in throwing the ball. Here and there a Benny Friedman of Michigan or a Swede Oberlander of Dartmouth might challenge the skeptics, but for the most part the pass was thought to be of use mainly as a weapon to loosen a defense that was crowding in and smothering the running game.

In a curious parallel to military strategy, an appreciation of aerial tactics now began to distract coaches from their preoccupation with the ground attack. Football had been through its period of trench warfare, when strategy consisted merely of running over guard, then over tackle. In that era a quarterback who called an end run was thought to be some kind of Bolshevik. But in the twenties deception and a speedy, wide-open running game began to replace the frontal assault.

The thirties saw a full flowering of great passers, with the Southwest Conference's Sammy Baugh and Davey O'Brien, both of Texas Christian, gaining the widest acclaim. Nearly every school began to look for an accurate thrower.

In this era of the single and double wingback formations, the passer was still required to be a good runner and kicker as well. The idea of having a quarterback concentrate strictly on ball handling and passing, which is a major tenet of the

modern T formation, had not yet taken hold. The triple-threat tailback was still the key man in the offenses of the thirties.

The most innovative attacking styles were found in the Southwest Conference, but all through the twenties and early thirties the good teams of the section could not win the national attention which they deserved. Their best players, as good as those anywhere, were likewise ignored by All-America selectors.

The Texas Aggies had, in 1927, a remarkable tailback of manifold talents, Joel Hunt. He was expert in every phase of the game, especially scoring, in which he registered 128 points. Hunt was easily the most valuable performer in the country, and should have been on every All-America team. He also would undoubtedly have been the Heisman Trophy winner if the award had existed then. Thirty years later the Aggies would get their Heisman Trophy winner in the person of John David Crow.

But when Texans who had seen Hunt in action told their counterparts in other sections, they were put down for exaggeration. The same fate awaited partisans of Ray Morrison's exciting Southern Methodist teams of the period. The Mustangs threw the ball all over the field, ran multiple hand-off plays, and generally drove defenses to distraction.

Francis Schmidt raised Texas Christian to the top of the league in the late twenties and early thirties with another offense based on intricate maneuvers and deft ball handling. He then went up to Columbus to do the same thing for Ohio State.

The most admired coach of the time, however, was Dana Xenophon Bible, who turned out unbeaten, untied, and un-scored-upon elevens at Texas A. & M. in 1917 and 1919 respectively. It was an astonishing achievement to produce even one such team, yet the Aggies were overlooked when the experts named the top squads.

The provincialism of its schedule no doubt helped to hide Texas A. & M.'s accomplishments. Bible decided in 1921 that he needed a game with some club which had impressed the East. Accordingly, he scheduled a postseason meeting

Alabama's Harry Gilmer rising
ten feet above it all. On a clear day
he could almost see forever.

with the Praying Colonels of Centre College, the team that had upset Harvard in the surprise of the year.

Centre, led by the colorful quarterback Bo McMillin and coached by the equally newsworthy Uncle Charlie Moran, had attracted a crowd of Eastern writers after it conquered Harvard, and they all fully expected the Kentuckians to roll over Bible's team with much less effort.

The Aggies upset the upsetters, however, and convinced the traveling wise men of the excellence of Southwestern football. But somehow the impression did not remain. It would have been necessary for the best Texas teams to have played the best from the East and Midwest if they had wanted national recognition. No conference team had yet ventured to the Rose Bowl either.

It was not until 1935 that the football world turned its full attention to a happening on a Southwestern gridiron, and when it did, Southern Methodist and Texas Christian responded with one of the sport's all-time classics.

Each team entered with ten straight victories. Texas Christian was led by Sammy Baugh, the best passer the Southwest had seen until then, and many think, the best anywhere— before or since. Southern Methodist placed its hopes on Bobby Wilson, a nervy open-field runner.

It was a free-wheeling offensive show, and late in the fourth quarter, with the score tied 14–14, came the play that the Southwest would talk about for years. S.M.U. had the ball on the T.C.U. 43-yard line, but it was fourth down with considerable yardage required. Here Wilson decided to gamble. Instead of punting, the Mustangs' Bob Finley threw the ball as far downfield as he could. Wilson, off at the snap like a sprinter, managed to arrive at the goal at the same time as the pass did. It looked for an instant as though the ball had been thrown too high to be caught, but Wilson made a leap born of pure desperation and came down with it, to the consternation of three T.C.U. defenders.

The touchdown made Wilson an S.M.U. immortal and sent the Mustangs to the Rose Bowl as champions of the Southwest Conference. The school's share of the Pasadena gate receipts paid off the mortgage on its stadium and caused

124

Don Hutson catching a pass. They called him the Alabama Antelope in deference to the way he moved after he received the ball.

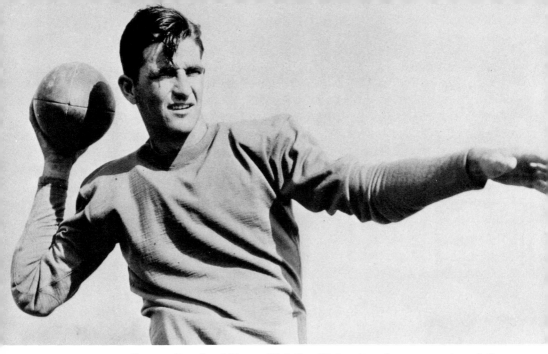

Sammy Baugh of Texas Christian University, the pass master of the Southwest—and every other direction on the compass before he was through.

many to refer to Wilson's great play as "the $85,000 catch."

T.C.U. was invited to the Sugar Bowl on the strength of its excellent showing, and there triumphed over Louisiana State.

Only one other Southwest Conference game since 1935 has been compared to the S.M.U.–T.C.U. epic and, oddly enough, it too was decided by a play much like Wilson's. The match in 1969 between perfect-record teams from Texas and Arkansas also drew the attention of the entire football world. Southwest historians immediately noted the parallels between the two famous games. In the 1969 encounter, however, Texas risked defeat rather than deadlock on its fourth-down pass play. The losing Arkansas team also went to the Sugar Bowl, but there the similarities to 1935 end. The Razorbacks lost at New Orleans, and Texas, instead of making a West Coast trip, went up the road a few miles to entertain Notre Dame in the Cotton Bowl.

Had there been a Cotton Bowl game on January 1, 1936, S.M.U. would have been much happier in it than the Mustangs were at Pasadena. Stanford's third successive Rose Bowl team finally won after having suffered defeats at the hands of Columbia and Alabama in the two preceding years. The last Vow Boys team, an experienced and highly motivated eleven, completely smothered the S.M.U. offense. Stanford scored only once itself, but that was enough for a 7–0 victory.

The S.M.U. performance was so lethargic that observers looked for some extenuating circumstance. Some thought that the Mustangs had exhausted themselves psychologically against T.C.U. Others held that the victory had bred over-confidence and that the S.M.U. players believed what they read in the Los Angeles press about Stanford being jinxed in the Rose Bowl.

Despite the temporary setback in prestige, however, the Southwest Conference had established its national reputation, and within a few years it would see two of its championship teams rise to the pinnacle of the gridiron.

14. "Show Me a Hero"

"Show me a hero," said F. Scott Fitzgerald, "and I will write you a tragedy." But his fellow Princetonians, at least those concerned with the Tigers' declining football fortunes, did not agree. There had been no heroes for them since long before the war, and that was reckoned as the tragedy.

It was not that Princeton had never known larger-than-life figures on the gridiron. There had been the mighty Hector Cowan back in the nineties, and those who had seen him against even the fabled Heffelfinger of Yale concluded that there had been little to choose between them.

And there had been all those Poes, including the one who said, "A team that won't be beat can't be beat." Not the best grammar perhaps—as one might expect of a Princeton man—but it did result in a victory over Yale, and for that most coveted of prizes any son of Old Nassau would gladly sacrifice his syntax.

There had been Snake Ames and Phil King, and in more recent years Hobey Baker and Sam White. To beat both Yale and Harvard on long runs late in the game, as White had done in 1911, was the dream of every Princeton football player. But for long years after White's storybook dashes, the Tigers knew only frustration, not to be relieved until after the war, when coach Bill Roper came back.

It had been under Roper that Princeton had ruled the East, and it did not take him long to turn out another champion. The 1922 Tiger eleven became known as the Team of Destiny. It won this accolade for a fourth-quarter performance against Chicago that ranks with the proudest in Princeton's history.

Stagg's Maroons led 18–7 in the last period on three touchdowns by their All-America fullback, John Thomas. Then Princeton capitalized on a Chicago fumble and scored. Moments later another touchdown was made. Princeton kicked both extra points and now led 21–18. All the Tigers had to do was hold the lead. But Chicago, cheered on by a huge Stagg Field crowd, came rushing down the field. On the big fourth-down play that meant the game, Princeton's line, led by All-America tackle Herb Treat, denied Thomas the winning touchdown. It was a performance worthy of Hector Cowan and the giants of old. Princeton's 3-point victory sent the Team of Destiny on to a perfect season and a share of the Eastern championship.

Cornell claimed the other half on the basis of a second perfect season in succession. The next year the Big Red again rolled over eight opponents to complete a spotless three-year cycle under Gil Dobie's painstaking direction.

These were the great Cornell teams led by Edgar Kaw and George Pfann, two of the best backs ever to play on the same varsity. Dobie brought the well-proven methods to Ithaca which had enabled him to dominate football in the Northwest before the war. His devotion to the running game and snappy blocking and tackling made Cornell's clubs far more proficient at the fundamentals than were their opponents.

But despite the awesome point totals of the three teams (392–21 in 1921, 339–27 in 1922, and 320–33 in 1923), there were still a number of critics who pointed out that Cornell had not played Harvard, Yale, or Princeton. The Eastern teams continued to form two distinct groups, members of which only rarely encountered each other. Cornell and Pennsylvania went one way, while the big three—Harvard, Yale, and Princeton—went another.

The result was considerable bickering over who was the best in the region where the game began. Dobie's detractors also continued to bemoan his failure to realize the utility of the forward pass. The dour perfectionist, however, brushed them all aside, went on refining his ground game, reading Schopenhauer, and, in accord with the pessimistic Teuton's world view, smiling seldom if at all.

Eventually, as it always does, the material declined, and the songs of jubilation that had echoed far above Cayuga's waters were replaced by choruses of derision. Dobie endured the steady erosion for another decade before departing, with the wry observation that "You can't win football games with Phi Beta Kappas."

But Dartmouth proved him wrong. The Indians from Hanover brought forth in the mid-twenties a varsity that was two-deep in Phi Beta Kappas and also better at playing football than anybody around. With the stunningly accurate Swede Oberlander throwing the ball, the Big Green went unbeaten in 1924, although tied by Yale.

The next year Oberlander's aerials annihilated unbeaten Cornell by a score of 62–13 in the game that established Dartmouth's claim to national recognition.

The Indians discovered early that Dobie's team could contain their running plays, and were resourceful enough to alter their strategy in favor of an overhead attack. But the proficiency of Oberlander at finding the gaps in the Cornell pass defense astounded even his own coach, Jesse Hawley. Six touchdowns were made through the air. And just to prove that he was not a one-game phenomenon, Oberlander passed a strong Chicago eleven into submission a week later at Stagg Field.

Dartmouth solved the tricky problem of its ancient Yale Bowl jinx by not playing the Elis in 1925. The Indians would have won easily, no doubt, but any other year they were not a good bet against Yale.

Football at New Haven had undergone a significant improvement after the war, with the return of Tad Jones to the coaching chair.

During his prewar tenure, Jones had managed to end the domination of Yale by Percy Haughton's Harvard. He was totally dedicated to winning, and told one of his teams: "Gentlemen, you are about to play a game of football against Harvard. Never again in your lives will you do anything as important."

130

Red Cagle of Army. In his day, he was Mr. Inside and Mr. Outside all in one.

He began to build a succession of strong, versatile elevens that culminated in the all-victorious 1923 champions. This was the squad which boasted such stars as All-America tackle Century Milstead and "Wild Bill" Mallory and Mal Stevens in the backfield. It shut out both Princeton and Harvard, all that any Yale man could ask of his team, and experienced serious trouble only with a Maryland club which it underrated. The Terrapins had the year's biggest upset within their grasp, but Yale demonstrated its class by rallying for a 2-point victory.

This was the last undefeated, untied Yale team for thirty-seven years. New Haven was still to see a number of good elevens and some classic individual performances, but the time when the Blue held unchallenged dominion over the gridiron was now part of history.

The glory was not all past, however, as those who saw the Yale–Army match in 1929 would testify. The Cadets swept into the packed Bowl heavily favored. They were led by their celebrated open-field runner, Christian Keener Cagle.

131

He had red hair and soon acquired the appropriate nickname. Many were comparing him to that other Red—Grange—and it did no disservice to the Galloping Ghost.

Cagle's was a sound Army team, like the others which had come from West Point since the war. Army seldom lost more than a game or two, usually to Notre Dame or an equally formidable opponent. Critics scoffed, however, at some of the small schools on the Army schedule, but the Cadet teams were still good ones.

Yale fell quickly behind by two touchdowns. Now the beleaguered home forces called upon a tiny halfback who weighed only 145 pounds and looked as though he should have been carrying water instead of the football. His name was Albie Booth, and in a Yale uniform he fit perfectly the nickname Little Boy Blue, which was to follow him throughout an exciting varsity career.

Booth, a New Haven native, responded to the cheers of the hometown crowd by running through the Army for a touchdown. Before the stunned Cadets could regroup, he came back and did it again with another brilliant dash. Consternation swept the Army ranks as Booth kicked the extra point that put Yale in the lead. But it was still anyone's game—that is, until Booth got his hands on the ball again. This time he took an Army punt on his 35-yard line and threaded his way down the field to the touchdown that broke West Point's spirit.

Booth was not particularly fast and had little power, but he had a clever change of pace and that indefinable sixth sense which all game-breaking runners seem to possess. Whatever equipment it took to contain him had not been issued to the troops that day.

Yale reveled in a 21–13 upset victory, and for years afterward garrulous Old Blues would peer into their brandy snifters and regale incredulous listeners with the tale of that Saturday in 1929. Little Boy Blue had outshone even the fabulous Red Cagle. But, unlike his nursery rhyme namesake, he would never be asked to blow his horn. Seventy thousand who were in the Yale Bowl that afternoon would always do it for him.

Albie Booth, Yale's Little Boy Blue.   133
Those who were there that day would
never forget. Those who weren't would
never quite understand.

Harvard had no player quite like Booth, except perhaps for the scintillating Barry Wood, but football did not expire at Cambridge after the great Haughton had stopped coaching. Indeed, in the seasons just after the war the Crimson put two of the best teams in its history on the gridiron. They were coached by Bob Fisher, twice an All-America guard on Haughton's championship teams. The big man in Fisher's offense was Eddie Casey, a dazzling all-round back who led Harvard to an undefeated season and a Rose Bowl victory in 1919.

The Crimson was unbeaten again the next year, but for the second straight time played a tie with Princeton. Harvard numbered among its victims in 1920 the Praying Colonels of Centre College. The Kentuckians were not the denigrated yokels that some accounts have led future generations to believe. Most Eastern experts knew that they played good football in Danville, and anyone could see that Alvin Nugent McMillin was almost a team all by himself.

Centre was invited back in 1921 on the strength of its good showing, the score of the 1920 encounter having been 31–14 in Harvard's favor. Despite the fact that few expected the Colonels to win the return match, any team with "Bo" McMillin in its backfield had to be conceded a fighting chance.

Both schools were undefeated when they met, although Harvard had been held to a tie by Penn State on the previous Saturday. The Crimson, moreover, was trying for its twenty-sixth game without a loss. But Bo McMillin ended the streak in one 32-yard burst for the game's only touchdown. Centre's tenacious defense repeatedly kept the Harvard backs from getting even and, much to the chagrin of all Cambridge and the East as well, the Colonels took home a 6–0 victory.

Historians have long disagreed over which was football's greatest upset, with some believing that the Illinois conquest of Minnesota in 1916 deserves the prize. Others hold out for Columbia over Stanford in the 1934 Rose Bowl, Navy over Army in 1950, Southern Cal over Notre Dame in 1964, Notre Dame over Oklahoma in 1957, Yale over Princeton in 1934, Columbia over Army in 1947, Purdue over Michigan

State in 1953, Holy Cross over Boston College in 1942, Great Lakes over Notre Dame in 1943, Dartmouth over Cornell in 1940, Illinois over Michigan in 1939, T.C.U. over Texas in 1941, or Michigan over Ohio State in 1969. These are only a few, however, and the argument is unending. But probably more experts think of Centre's victory over Harvard, when the word "upset" is mentioned, than of any other surprise outcome on the gridiron.

Football dominance had passed from the East to the provinces, notably the Midwest, as the twenties gave way to the thirties. Nevertheless there were still many first-rate players—of whom Ken Strong of New York University, the country's leading scorer in 1928, may have been the best— and now and then a nationally ranked team in the region where the game began.

Harvard could still draw a full house at Michigan's vast stadium when it ventured West for the first time, in 1929. And the Crimson could also point proudly to the anchor of its line, Ben Ticknor, the best center in college football.

But probably no single game revived the sagging prestige of the East as much as Columbia's stunning upset of Stanford in the 1934 Rose Bowl. The Lions were not really so weak a team as an observer might have supposed after the gasp that went up when the final score became known. But they were not the best in their section, and this was one reason why the West Coast sportswriters downgraded them so cruelly.

Princeton was the class of the East, with a perfect record, which included a three-touchdown win over Columbia. That, however, was the only game the Lions had lost. They were a light, fast, resourceful club, coached by Lou Little, a teacher comparable to Amos Alonzo Stagg in that he worked near-miracles with unprepossessing material.

The West Coast was not impressed with an also-ran, however. It had Stanford's Vow Boys, and the only opponents deemed good enough were either Michigan's Big Ten (and national) champions or Princeton.

When Columbia arrived, the Coast writers called it "Pomona High School in light-blue jerseys." This was all a master psychologist of Lou Little's caliber needed. Motivation was no longer any problem for the Easterners, but overconfidence was becoming one for Stanford.

Little did not leave everything to bruised egos, however. He armed the Lions with one dazzling reverse play, the legendary KF-79, in which quarterback Cliff Montgomery slipped the ball to fullback Al Barabas. There was elaborate faking, especially by the artful Montgomery, and Barabas proceeded around the Stanford right side for 17 yards and a touchdown. The Indians had been confused momentarily and then blocked before they could recover.

A muddy field slowed both offenses, but after the early touchdown it was Columbia's refusal to yield on defense that really spelled Stanford's downfall. A 7-point lead against a team as strong as the Vow Boys could not have endured without a magnificent effort at containment. This is exactly what Little got from his angry Lions, with a monumental assist from the West Coast sportswriters.

The biggest upset in Rose Bowl history sent Eastern stock soaring, but what kept it up for a few more years, at least, was the record made by the Princeton teams under coach Herbert Orin "Fritz" Crisler. As soon as Stagg's chief assistant had arrived from the Big Ten, it seemed as though every good prep school football player in the East was trudging in the direction of Nassau Hall with a copy of *This Side of Paradise* under his arm.

Before Crisler's arrival some disastrous seasons had brought the Tigers to low ebb, the crowning indignity of which had been a 51–14 drubbing at Yale's hands.

With Crisler came not only gifted athletes but a seemingly inexhaustible store of brilliantly designed offensive maneuvers. As he would show in even greater detail at Michigan, Fritz Crisler had perfected the techniques of offensive football beyond anything yet seen. He always acknowledged a debt to Harvard's innovative single wing strategist Dick Harlow, but anyone who watched Crisler's elevens, either at Princeton or at Ann Arbor, knew that they exhibited the handiwork of a rare and independent intellect.

Princeton took a year to adjust to Crisler's teachings, then stormed over every opponent in 1933 with such a com-

136

bination of power, finesse, and opportunism that only 8 points were allowed all season, while 217 were scored.

Crisler did not subscribe to the idea of playing strictly for the other team's mistakes. He was too good at designing plays that moved the ball to accept so defensive an orientation. Yet his best teams at Princeton and all ten of his Michigan clubs were superb on defense. Crisler always doted on timing, and if this was indispensable to his precision offense, it turned out to be almost as helpful for defensive maneuvers as well.

With All-America tackle Charles Ceppi and guard John Weller in the line, and such backfield stars as Pepper Constable, Garry LeVan, and Paul Pauk, the Tigers won every game but one in the years 1933–34–35. The defeat, 7–0, by Larry Kelley and his inspired Yale teammates in 1934 was as crushing to Princeton as it was satisfying to the Blue. It was the greatest upset in the ninety-two-game rivalry between the two old enemies.

But the Tigers came back the next season with perhaps an even better team than the one of 1933 and took revenge by humbling the Elis 38–7. The 1935 Princeton team, after a close contest with Pennsylvania, proceeded to intimidate everyone else on its schedule.

The two unbeaten elevens were the best that the school had turned out in more than thirty years. And Fritz Crisler had become perhaps the most honored resident of Old Nassau since Woodrow Wilson.

Dartmouth too regained its championship form during the thirties, under the meticulous direction of Colonel Earl H. Blaik. The Big Green succeeded in ending the Yale Bowl jinx, going unbeaten in 1937 and producing an All-America back in the person of Bob MacLeod, who was so good that the old-timers around Hanover were reminded of the superlative Myles Lane.

Blaik was perhaps the best organized coach in the history of the game. He planned every minute of practice with the foresight that one might expect of a no-nonsense West Pointer. Everyone in Hanover knew that the Army would someday call Blaik back to the plains above the Hudson.

Football at the Academy had declined drastically, and when Cornell and Pennsylvania decimated the Cadets in the same season, the word went out to recall the Colonel.

Blaik had attended Miami University in Oxford, Ohio, before entering West Point. Miami has been known as a preparatory school for some of the best coaches in football. Paul Brown, Sid Gillman, Ara Parseghian, Paul Dietzel, John Pont, Woody Hayes, Bo Schembechler, and Stu Holcomb have all either coached or played at the school.

Blaik's most unusual experience at Dartmouth, and one of the oddest imaginable, occurred in the 1940 Cornell game. The Indians had a magnificent 3–0 upset in their grasp when Cornell, unbeaten in seventeen encounters, made a last desperate drive to salvage the game. After fourth down, with only seconds to go, near Dartmouth's goal, the Cornell bid apparently had failed. But referee Red Friesell became confused and awarded an extra down to the Big Red. With time having all but expired, Cornell scored and went to its dressing room with a 6–3 victory.

Many writers covering the game, however, and a number of Dartmouth men, were certain that an error had been committed. Because of the pandemonium that had reigned in the final minutes as Cornell moved toward the Dartmouth goal, it had been impossible for the officials to confer calmly. Later, though, when motion pictures revealed the fifth down, Cornell, in one of the most sportsmanlike actions in the annals of football, relinquished its victory and saw its undefeated streak end. There was no way for Dartmouth to have won the game, in spite of the official's mistake, unless Cornell had so willed it.

The season before, however, Cornell had needed no help from the referee in demolishing eight opponents on the way to a perfect record. Indeed, there were many who thought that the 1939 Big Red team was the best in the nation. Much support for this view came after the Easterners defeated Big Ten champion Ohio State at Columbus in the most exciting game of the year.

The Buckeyes appeared far superior in the early moments, and took a two-touchdown lead. Then, in an instant, Cornell

Red Blaik of Army. They called him "the MacArthur of the Gridiron," but this was one old soldier who wouldn't fade away.

struck, with tailback Walt Scholl exploding for a long scoring run. Before the dizzy Ohioans could compose themselves, another one-play touchdown had put Cornell back in the game.

Ohio State had made its scores the hard way, by sustained marches. To see their carefully attained lead melt away in two lightning strokes unhinged the Buckeyes, and Cornell went on to a convincing 23–14 victory.

Carl Snavely was the coach who directed the Big Red during its banner seasons in the thirties. He had such All-America players as Jerome "Brud" Holland at end and Nick Drahos at tackle, in addition to backfield men of the caliber of Scholl and Mort Landsberg.

Although no one in the East could foresee it at the time, the 1939 Cornell team would be the last of the old Establishment elevens to be seriously considered for a national championship.

There were other teams in 1939, of course. Texas A. & M. was the popular choice as number one, with Southern Cali-

139

fornia also favored in some quarters. But Cornell's claim was more than respectable, especially in view of its victory over Ohio State. There was, at any rate, not much doubt that these were the three best elevens of the season.

Despite the decline of their relative team strength, however, the old leaders in the East still would turn out some great players, and their traditional rivalries would continue with as much spirit as ever.

15. Critical Spirits

Between the crash and Pearl Harbor stretched the decade-long hangover known as the Great Depression. The social criticism which grew out of it affected nearly every American institution, even one as relatively frivolous as college football.

Some of those who looked closely at the game discovered that it was violent, venal, and vulgar. If these were harsh judgments, what made them all but unbearable to most people, who took the sport as it came, was that they were so often undeniably true.

But instead of simply admitting this and then trying as best they could to curb its more rampant abuses, many of the defenders wrapped themselves and football in the flag and protested loudly that any criticism of the game was a criticism of the country as well.

An occasional cynic accepted the muckrakers' view of football with the observation that it gave precisely the right training to those about to enter the society beyond graduation. But for the most part, however, the game was held, by the vast majority, to be as American as cherry pie.

Perhaps the most searing indictment of football had come years before, in 1905, from Dr. Charles W. Eliot, president of Harvard, who wrote: "Death and injuries are not the strongest arguments against football . . . that cheating and brutality are profitable is the main evil."

Those schools which did choose to abandon the sport, however, generally based their action not on ethical but, rather, on economic grounds. Supporting a big-time football program is an expensive undertaking, which yields financial gain only if the school is adept at filling its stadium.

That the game has survived in nearly all of the great academic centers, as well as in those of more modest cerebral attainments, suggests that there may be something in football which is fundamental to the American campus mentality, or perhaps, more accurately, alumni mentality.

Both critics and defenders of the game agreed that as far as eligibility standards, conduct on the field, and coaching methods went, there had been a considerable improvement over conditions in the nineties.

The tramp athlete was largely a creature of the past. Many schools were even making some effort to help struggling players surmount their classroom difficulties by hiring tutors. This application of the principle that "strong minds think so that weak minds may pass" kept more than one halfback on the varsity. Less enlightened institutions, however, merely herded their Hessians into basket weaving or some similar subject.

The prevailing public impression of football players continued to be that they lacked intellect, and there always seemed to be enough examples around to support the generalization. Yet this was unfair to the large number of collegians who managed the difficult feat of being both a varsity member and a serious scholar in a respectable discipline.

It was impossible to tell how many fit into this category. The all-out defender of the game insisted that nearly every player did, while the all-out detractor allowed for only a few. Also insoluble was the riddle of whether the time and energy expended on the gridiron added or subtracted from one's university experience.

Undoubtedly, an intelligent athlete could learn numerous lessons in applied psychology and group dynamics by taking part in football. But just as undoubtedly, he would have to forego enlightenment in other areas. The all-out critic seldom acknowledged that any mental enlargement other than a swelled head could result from playing the game. But there seemed enough disputants to blunt the edge of at least this one criticism.

Still, the ethical corruptions and the ego distortions, which infected especially the most sought-after players, did dismay those who chose to confront them honestly.

It could well be the case that the athletes who benefit most from football, except financially, are those on the third or fourth strings, or the reserves. They learn the fundamentals, experience the emotions attendant upon both winning and losing, appreciate the few moments they appear in the games, and emerge from the whole process with probably a healthier self-awareness than does the star. No one has yet tested this hypothesis, but perhaps some doctoral candidate is even now laboring over a questionnaire.

16. Gophers, Panthers, and Other Animals

Two coaches with virtually the same approach to football dominated the game in the thirties. Bernie Bierman of Minnesota and Jock Sutherland of Pittsburgh were both fanatics in their devotion to precision blocking and tackling.

For the most part, the Gophers and the Panthers went their separate ways. But one afternoon in 1934, when each may well have fielded the finest of all its squads, they clashed head-on before a jammed house at Pitt Stadium. What happened was perhaps the all-time classic example of power football. There was little finesse in either offense, yet, strangely, the play that decided the game was a bit of uncharacteristic razzle-dazzle that Bierman had dreamed up on the train.

Minnesota was at the beginning of an unmatched championship cycle, during which it would win six Big Ten titles in eight years, negotiate four seasons perfectly, and claim national preeminence no less than five times.

Gopher football tradition seemed to dictate that only players of the dimensions of a Bronko Nagurski could wear the Maroon and Gold. Nagurski, the school's most famous athlete, had starred in the late twenties at three positions: end, tackle, and fullback. At 6'2" and 220 pounds, he had not been the biggest man in the game by any means, but he seemed to have been the most devastating. It is doubtful if any player who ever lived could have handled so many aspects of line and backfield play so well.

Some idea of Nagurski's impression upon the experts can

Bernie Bierman of Minnesota. They called him the Silver Fox, and his Golden Gophers claimed five national championships in the years from 1934 until the war.

be gained from the fact that he is the only superstar who is placed at either tackle or fullback on many of the all-time teams. He ran, blocked, and tackled peerlessly, and this is exactly what Bernie Bierman demanded of the aspirants who arrived at Minneapolis in the thirties.

That he got what he wanted is a matter of record. The ability of players such as Butch Larson at end, Ed Widseth and Dick Smith at tackles, Bill Bevan at guard, and a backfield composed of Glen Seidel at quarterback, Pug Lund and Julie Alphonse at the halfbacks, and Stan Kostka at fullback was enough to ensure that the 1934 Minnesota team was one of the finest in the history of football.

It was just the kind of club that was perfectly fitted to Bierman's philosophy of coaching. Eleven Nagurskis could not have made his system work any better. Eight straight victories were achieved, with a point score of 270–38.

In the Pitt game, the Gophers gave up a surprise touchdown on a quick opening dash by Izzy Weinstock, one of

145

the best in a long line of great Panther fullbacks. As the game moved into the last quarter, Minnesota's depth and power were forcing Pitt into a continually deteriorating field position, but still the score was 7–0 in favor of the home team. Suddenly a fumbled punt enabled the Gophers to move in for the tying touchdown. Now it was a new game, with the momentum all on Minnesota's side and time running out. Pitt's only hope was to advance the ball, use up the remaining minutes, and settle for a tie, but the Gopher defense thwarted this strategy and regained possession.

With the 230-pound Kostka hammering repeatedly into the Pitt line, Minnesota moved inexorably down the field. It became apparent that unless the Panthers contained Kostka, they would be undone. But line plunges take up time, and now Bierman began to worry over whether these maneuvers could beat the clock.

He decided that they could not and, with the ball still 30 yards from the goal, sent in the play of the year. Kostka lumbered toward the line. Pitt massed to stop him, but at the last moment the big fullback slipped the ball to Seidel. Seidel then lateraled it to Lund, who threw a long pass downfield for the winning touchdown.

The play was called the "buck lateral." The brilliant maneuver had endless variations. The fullback could simply keep the ball, or the quarterback could run, pass, hand it to a crossing wingback, or, as Seidel had done, lateral it to his tailback. The tailback, especially if he could run and pass skillfully, presented an almost insoluble problem for the defense.

When a team had the crushing power of Minnesota, moreover, the buck-lateral series was even more effective, since the opposing line had to converge on the charging fullback. The instant it did that, it left its flanks vulnerable. If the defensive halfbacks made the mistake of rushing in to help stop the apparent ballcarrier, the secondary was left wide open for a long pass.

But, as every coach knows, the most intricate plays on paper will not work on the field without superior personnel to execute them. After the Second World War Bierman was still just as fine a coach and the buck lateral still a sensational weapon, but Minnesota's talent had declined, and no invention could remedy that condition.

In the mid-thirties, however, some coaches felt that any formation Bierman chose would be unstoppable. Perhaps that might have been true in cases where the opponent was outclassed, but the big victory over Pitt showed that the Gophers could be as good at deception as they were at straight power.

In 1935, although beset by a plague of injuries, Minnesota again won all eight games. A fierce goal-line stand in the last minute saved the day against Nebraska, and Northwestern was subdued only with the greatest difficulty.

The Wildcats, coached by Lynn "Pappy" Waldorf, fielded some of their strongest teams in the middle and late thirties. Their games with Minnesota were all extremely close, with the biggest margin being only 8 points. They were taut defensive struggles, in which a touchdown usually was enough to ensure victory.

If it had not been for Waldorf's 1936 Northwestern team, Minnesota would have accomplished the almost impossible feat of going through three consecutive perfect seasons. No Big Ten team has ever done this.

During the first month of the campaign it seemed as though the Gophers would be even better than they had been in 1934. New players had moved up to fill the vacancies created by graduation, but still the talent was prodigious.

At quarterback Bierman had installed the supremely resourceful Charles "Bud" Wilkinson, later to become one of the great coaches in history. Wilkinson had played guard during the two previous seasons, and his blocking ability was perfectly suited to the quarterback position in Bierman's single wing. Wilkinson's daring lateral to Andy Uram on a punt return in the last minute of the Nebraska game turned an apparent scoreless tie into a 7–0 Minnesota victory.

When the Gophers arrived in Evanston, however, for the crucial game with Northwestern, they faced an opponent which was at a near-manic emotional level. A muddy field made it certain that there would be little scoring, but, as

147

observers of this bitter rivalry well knew, there had not been many points made even on dry fields in years past.

The devotees of defensive football were not disappointed, as the two perfectly matched machines rumbled into the fourth quarter with the score 0–0. That would have been the final result if Northwestern had not driven deep into Minnesota territory and, just when it appeared to have been halted, received the break of the year: a 15-yard penalty against the Gophers for unnecessary roughness. The ball was placed on the one, and Northwestern quickly pushed it across for a 6–0 victory which gave it the Big Ten championship.

This ought to have given the Wildcats the mythical national title as well. The Associated Press had begun its poll of sportswriters to determine the country's best eleven. Northwestern, however, fell before twice-beaten Notre Dame in its final game. The Irish seemed unawed by the prestige which the Purple had gained as "the team that stopped Minnesota." They outplayed Northwestern in every phase of the game and won easily by three touchdowns.

When the experts chose the season's number one team, Minnesota was given the prize. It seemed incongruous that a club which could not win its own conference championship should be called the best in the nation, but even more bizarre happenings were to feature the wire-service polls through the years.

Bierman's teams of 1937 and 1938 regained the Big Ten title, but lost twice each season. Notre Dame won a pair of games, Nebraska finally managed to beat a Bierman team, and Waldorf's Northwestern gained a close decision.

After an off year in 1939 the Gophers were ready to end their championship cycle in grand style. They rolled through the last two seasons before the war undefeated and untied. Two more national championships were their reward.

In 1940 they played four opponents which were rated among the top ten in the final wire-service poll. No other strong team of that season encountered such rugged opposition.

These champion teams had the Bierman trademark—great tackles—in the persons of Dick Wildung and Urban Odson.

149

Bronko Nagurski of Minnesota. Runner,
blocker, and tackler beyond comparison,
here he takes a fling as a passer too.

They had versatile, speedy halfbacks, such as Bruce Smith and George Franck, and they had the pulverizing line plunger, Bill Daley, that was essential to the power single wing. But they did not win their games by the overpowering scores of earlier years. In fact, they were fortunate to win the 1941 Northwestern game at all. The Wildcats had lost by a point the year before in a typical Bierman–Waldorf battle of attrition, but this time they seemed to be in command.

Minnesota, with the ball near midfield, ran a play and then appeared slow in returning to its huddle. Several of the Gopher linemen chatted amiably with their Northwestern counterparts—for a moment it seemed as though someone were about to serve tea—when the ball was suddenly snapped to Bud Higgins, a halfback. He sped away from all the conversation and ran for a touchdown while Northwestern appealed to the referee.

The protest was in vain, however, for the officials had been carefully forewarned that Minnesota would spring its "talking play." The maneuver was perfectly legal in that seven men were on the line of scrimmage when the ball was snapped and no backfield man was moving forward. The touchdown wiped out a 7–2 Northwestern lead, and gave the Gophers another 1-point victory.

Beating Northwestern was only one of the keys to the success of Minnesota's championship teams. All through the decade they humbled Michigan as well. In the mid-thirties that was no problem, since the Wolverines fell into their worst depression during 1934–37, and were annihilated by Ohio State as well as by the Gophers.

After Fritz Crisler arrived at Ann Arbor in 1938, however, Minnesota was almost the only team that could beat Michigan. In 1938, 1940, and 1941 the Gophers won twice by a point and once by a touchdown, in each case ruining an undefeated season for the Wolverines.

From 1933 to 1941 Minnesota's record under Bierman showed 58 victories against only 9 defeats, 4 of which came in 1939. The two consecutive perfect seasons have been equaled by Michigan's teams of 1947 and 1948, but by no other Big Ten school since. The domination of the wire-service polls exercised by the Gophers has been matched

John Bain Sutherland, D.D.S., (left) watches with an assistant as his Pittsburgh Panthers loosen the teeth of some hapless opponent one afternoon in 1934.

only by the Notre Dame teams of the late forties.

What Minnesota was to the Big Ten, Pittsburgh was to Eastern football: the team to beat. Jock Sutherland had turned out superior elevens all through the late twenties and early thirties, but it was in the last five years of his coaching tenure that the Panthers reached their peak.

There was even a Rose Bowl victory, which nearly allowed the Pitt faithful to forget the grief their 1929 and 1932 teams had come to in Pasadena. Sutherland had never quite recovered from the two catastrophes at Southern California's hands, and it was with some trepidation that he took Pitt to the 1937 Rose Bowl to meet a tough Washington team. But he need not have worried. Pittsburgh was far too strong for the Huskies and won by three touchdowns.

As good as the Panthers were in the mid-thirties, however, they never achieved a perfect season. They lost one game in 1933, 1934, 1935, and 1936. The defeats were each by only a few points: by 4 to Minnesota in 1933, by 6 to Minnesota in the famous 1934 game, by 3 to Notre Dame in 1935, and by 7 to Duquesne in 1936.

In 1937 the Panthers, with perhaps their best team ever, went through without a loss, led by the great fullback Marshall Goldberg. These were the years of the Dream Backfield, which also included John Chickerneo, Dick Cassiano, and Harold Stebbins.

Pitt fans argued happily among themselves over whether this was a better unit than the Rose Bowl quartet of the previous season: John Michelosen (later Pitt's coach), Goldberg, Bobby LaRue, and Frank Patrick. The key to both backfields was the unstoppable Goldberg, who has been named to many all-time teams as a running back.

But in spite of such ball-carrying talent, Pitt could not score a point for three consecutive years against the Fordham Rams of coach Jim Crowley.

The fact that Fordham could not score a point on Pitt either made for one of the most remarkable occurrences in the annals of the sport. In 1935, 1936, and 1937 the two schools played to 0–0 ties. The 1937 game matched perfect records, and both teams went on from the deadlock to win the rest of their games. It was a case, for three seasons, of the irresistible force meeting the immovable object.

Pitt's awesome running game, in which Sutherland massed interference so crushingly ahead of his deep reverse that the old-timers thought the flying wedge had returned, piled up on the rocks of Fordham's celebrated Seven Blocks of Granite.

The Rams were led by Ed Franco and Alexander Wojciechowicz, whose name Pitt could neither pronounce nor forget. He seemed to know exactly where the Panthers were going on every play and just how to keep them from getting there.

All the Fordham linemen were good. They had a perfectionist named Frank Leahy drilling them. Leahy had served as Crowley's line coach at Michigan State, and accompanied the famous Horseman to Rose Hill.

Crowley, as head coach, was anything but the "Sleepy Jim" that Rockne had christened him at Notre Dame. He was an imaginative and resourceful teacher with much of Rockne's psychological insight. Under his direction Fordham achieved its greatest football successes.

If Fordham managed to check the mighty Panthers, few other teams did. In the fifteen seasons that Sutherland coached, Pitt won 111 games and lost only 20. This remarkable record was all the more impressive in view of the difficult schedules which were played.

In the mid-thirties Pitt took on Notre Dame, Ohio State, Duke, Nebraska, Army, Southern California, and Navy in addition to such traditional rivals as Carnegie Tech, Duquesne, Penn State, Syracuse, and West Virginia.

Against the Irish, Sutherland enjoyed a 5–3 advantage, one of the few coaches to hold a winning percentage over the dominant team in the game. Pitt's persecution of Notre Dame teams from 1932 through 1937, during which time it won five out of six games, resulted in a break in relations between the two schools. Coach Elmer Layden of the Irish freely admitted that he was tired of having his clubs pulverized by the Panthers. Sutherland seemed to have the knack of keying Pitt to its best game of the season when it went against Notre Dame. The victory margins were not that humiliating, but the manner in which the Irish were outplayed was.

Sutherland had learned his lessons well from Pop Warner while starring on his pre-World War I Pitt teams. Although never exhibiting the inventive genius of his famed coach, Sutherland nonetheless turned out high-scoring elevens.

Defensively they were equaled only by Bierman's Minnesota teams, whose dedication to fundamentals matched their own. In his obsession with blocking and tackling and a simple but flawlessly executed offense, Sutherland reminded observers of Gilmour Dobie. Some also saw a similarity in personalities, both men being of Scottish background, reserved in temperament, and tireless in their attention to detail.

153

Sutherland was able to combine his coaching duties with a career as a lecturer in dentistry at the university, an odd contrast in professions, which caused some opponents to wonder whether he wanted subconsciously to make amends for the damage his teams did each Saturday.

There was one coach who knew what it was to face both Sutherland and Bierman during these years. He was Dana X. Bible, who had come to Nebraska from Texas A. & M. in 1929. The Cornhusker teams turned out by this excellent teacher dominated their conference, which was then the Big Six but has since become the Big Eight. Nebraska, in fact, would have enjoyed six unbeaten seasons but for defeats by either Minnesota or Pittsburgh.

Two of the best backs in the country, George Sauer and Sam Francis, led Bible's clubs to consistently high national ratings. He returned to the Southwest Conference in 1937 to restore the depleted reputation of the University of Texas, but the Cornhuskers kept on winning, under the able leadership of former West Pointer Biff Jones. They even managed to beat Minnesota twice, and at the end of the 1940 season they made the school's only visit to the Rose Bowl.

Bierman and Sutherland may have been at the top of their profession in the thirties, but they were not the only coaches who directed perfect-record teams.

Harry Kipke, at Michigan, brought the Yostian "a punt, a pass, and a prayer" philosophy to another glorious flowering, in which four straight Big Ten titles and two national championships were won.

The Wolverine team of 1932 was led by quarterback Harry Newman, a stocky, multitalented field general who possessed unerring accuracy as a forward passer and who seemed always to come up with the big play just when it was needed.

This was never better illustrated than in the tense struggle with Minnesota in the snow at Minneapolis. Newman kicked a field goal for the game's only points to give Michigan its perfect season. It was the crowning achievement of a brilliant three-year career during which Newman was the key to Michigan's offense.

Kipke, his coach, had fully imbibed Yost's football wis-

154

dom while starring as a halfback and punter in the early twenties. Kipke may have been the finest punter of his era, and an appreciation of the kicking game remained with him after he took over at Ann Arbor in 1929. He developed tough, agile defensive lines with such stars as Maynard Morrison, Ivan Williamson (later a highly successful coach at Wisconsin), and Francis Wistert.

The material fitted Kipke's system so perfectly that even after Newman graduated, Michigan still rolled along undefeated. The 1933 team again claimed the national title, although it was held to a scoreless tie by Minnesota.

The defensive skills of the 1932 and 1933 Wolverines may be measured by the fact that they allowed only two and three touchdowns respectively through the entire seasons.

Wistert was the bulwark of the line in 1933. He played tackle, wore the number 11, and was named to the All-America team. Nine years later his brother Albert played tackle, wore the number 11, and also won All-America honors. In 1949 his brother Alvin, not to be outdone, accomplished the same feat. Thus there were three brothers, each wearing the number 11, each playing the same position at the same university, and each earning All-America recognition. Princeton may have had her Poes and Notre Dame her Millers, but no family could quite match the Wisterts of Michigan, and their alma mater showed its gratitude by retiring the number 11.

Purdue had its best teams during the late twenties and early thirties. There had been a time when the phrase "Stagg fears Purdue" had been a sports-page joke, but now no one was laughing.

The Boilermakers had a perfect season in 1929 and were unbeaten but tied in 1932. Their coach was another of Rockne's former linemen, Noble Kizer. It was his bad luck, however, that Michigan was turning out teams which were just a bit better. When the two met in 1930 with the conference title as the prize, Newman passed and kicked the Wolverines to a 14–13 victory.

Ohio State also came alive again during the early thirties after the arrival of Francis Schmidt from the Southwest Conference. He had made Texas Christian the dominant power in that wild league with a razzle-dazzle offense that featured multiple ball handling and laterals all over the field. Schmidt instituted the same system at Columbus, and before long the Buckeyes were rolling up huge scores. His lack of compassion for outclassed opponents gave rise to the nickname "Close the Gates of Mercy," which followed the big Nebraskan throughout his career.

In the course of his travels, Schmidt had picked up a law degree, and he had the barrister's command of logic as well as invective. He imparted the intricacies of his offense with the skill of a lawyer arguing a case, emphasizing versatility to the extent that he taught all four starting backs to throw and catch passes.

If Schmidt neglected any phase of the game, it was defense. His conception of winning football simply did not fit in with the Yostian or Neylandian theory of capitalizing upon the opponent's errors. For Schmidt the real joy in coaching was to see one of his bewildering maneuvers executed with precision.

In 1935 he saw this often, as the Buckeyes swept past four adversaries and prepared to entertain Notre Dame's likewise unbeaten team in the first meeting between the schools.

17. One for the Book

Everyone knew that it would be the game of the year. Sportswriters poured into Columbus as they never had before, and a national radio network was set up to broadcast the event. It appeared for a while that nothing that would happen on the football field could possibly justify such massive preparations. After the game, however, it seemed that mere words, even the millions printed and spoken, had been almost totally inadequate to describe it.

For three quarters it was all Ohio State. The big Buckeye line, led by All-America center Gomer Jones, pushed Notre Dame around practically at will. An intercepted pass, followed by a deft lateral, yielded one touchdown, and a long march another. A reserve halfback named Dick Beltz kicked one extra point. The score was 13–0 in favor of the home team as the last period began.

Notre Dame, sensing that its only chance lay in throwing the ball, now opened up a furious aerial barrage with Andy Pilney passing to Frank Gaul, Wally Fromhart, and Wayne Millner.

Ohio State had never been a good defensive team against passes, and coach Francis Schmidt, in an effort to cope with the emergency, took a calculated risk. He withdrew his regular defensive backfield and inserted the second unit. Under the rules at that time a player who left the game could not return in the same period. Thus Ohio State was gambling that its more rested reserves would be better able to stop Notre Dame's desperation passes than would its starters. It was a logical move, for which Schmidt was willing to answer when the armchair quarterbacks along High Street raised their ex post facto objections.

But Pilney passed with sensational skill, and soon the Irish had a touchdown. The extra-point attempt failed. There were five minutes left when he got another chance to throw, and again he made the most of it. Notre Dame moved in for a second touchdown, but once more the conversion attempt went awry.

The huge Ohio State audience relaxed, knowing that only a minute remained and that all the home team had to do was hold onto the ball. The margin of victory would then be the extra point which Dick Beltz had made. In a minute he would be one of the Buckeyes' greatest football heroes.

Notre Dame did the only thing it could do under the circumstances: it tried an onside kick, but Ohio State claimed the ball near midfield. On the first play from scrimmage, however, Beltz ran wide, was tackled fiercely by the frantic Irish line, and fumbled. Notre Dame recovered.

Now Pilney faded quickly back to pass. He looked far down the field for someone to throw the ball to, but the Buckeye defenders covered every potential receiver. Undaunted, Pilney swept down the sideline for 32 vital yards, finally being thrown out of bounds on the Ohio State 19. In falling, he twisted his knee and had to be taken from the field on a stretcher.

There was bedlam in the Notre Dame stands and something approaching a mass rite of supplication among the Buckeye faithful as William Shakespeare came in to replace Pilney. Only thirty seconds remained in the game.

Shakespeare wasted no time in going to the air. He pitched the ball in the direction of his right halfback, Victor Wojcihovski, but it was badly aimed, and out of the deep secondary suddenly flashed Dick Beltz. He had 90 yards of open field ahead of him if he wanted a touchdown, but that was not really necessary. An interception, even without a yard's runback, would have sealed Notre Dame's fate and atoned for his fumble.

Beltz and the ball came together for an instant, and to

Ohio State–Notre Dame, 1935. Touchdown for the Irish, but they couldn't kick the extra point, and it is still 13–12 Buckeyes with only a minute left to play.

the Ohio State partisans, it seemed as though only some caprice of the gods could have jarred it from his desperate grasp. The ball fell to the ground—Much Ado About Nothing—and Shakespeare had been granted one more chance.

This time the bard of South Bend lofted the ball far beyond the Ohio State goal line with a last faint hope that All's Well That Ends Well. Wayne Millner raced under it at full speed, leaped high into the air, and clutched the victory in his outstretched hands. A lone Ohio State defender lunged hopelessly after him. It was Dick Beltz. An instant later the game was over. Notre Dame 18, Ohio State 13. The ecstatic Irish fans streamed onto the field, swept up their heroes, and tore down the goal posts.

The vast majority of the 81,000, however, sat in silent disbelief. The mighty Scarlet Scourge, one of the greatest elevens in Buckeye history, had lost a game that seemed securely in its possession only fifteen minutes before. But even in their despair, the Ohio State followers knew that they had seen one of the classics in the history of the game. Sportswriters, who had watched monumental confrontations of years past, nodded in agreement. This indeed had been one for the book.

For Dick Beltz, though, it had been pure Shakespearean tragedy. His fumble had given Notre Dame the ball. His dropped interception had allowed the Irish one last chance. And, as the final blow, the winning pass had been completed over his head. What made all this even more poignant, however, was the fact that Beltz had stood to be the hero by virtue of his successful conversion. Seldom in the annals of football has a player been the victim of such a cruel reversal of fortune—and all in the final sixty seconds.

Yet in a curious way Beltz was to know, in that eternal moment, the deepest meaning of an athlete's experience. He could not consciously have realized it in the turmoil of the instant, but he had achieved a communion with the victors and the vanquished of the ages. He had been privileged, as few men have, and at a fearful cost, to dwell in both Valhalla and Hades—all in the last flicker of the scoreboard clock.

160

Dick Beltz of Ohio State. First he heard the cheering; then he heard the silence.

18. General Bob and His Volunteers

The victory over Ohio State was the highlight of Notre Dame football during the thirties. Coach Elmer Layden did an excellent job, which, at any other school, would have been called sensational. From 1934 to 1940 his teams won 47 and lost 13 against some of the strongest elevens in the nation.

But Layden had the misfortune to fall between Rockne and Frank Leahy, who were not merely the most successful coaches in Notre Dame's history but in the entire history of football as well.

Layden's teams, moreover, were rudely treated by Jock Sutherland's Pittsburgh Panthers, an embarrassment which caused considerable grumbling among Notre Dame alumni. The Irish also lost big games to Southern California in 1938 and 1939, and to Iowa in 1939 and 1940. Even after their incredible triumph over Ohio State in 1935, the glory lasted for only a week. Northwestern pulled a monumental upset, winning by a touchdown. Layden and the Irish managed to return the compliment a year later, however, knocking the Wildcats out of a national championship.

The closest that Notre Dame came to a perfect season under Layden was in 1938, when the first eight opponents—including Army, Navy, Carnegie Tech, Minnesota, and Northwestern—were defeated. Only four touchdowns had been allowed by an unusually good Notre Dame defense, but in the season's finale with Southern California, the Irish failed to score and were defeated by two touchdowns.

162

This was the best Trojan team in years, one that Howard Jones would take to the Rose Bowl to face the unscored-upon Duke Blue Devils. But Notre Dame partisans were still bitterly disappointed. They wanted, at the very least, either a national championship or a perfect season—and preferably both. Rockne had so accustomed them to all-conquering elevens that a coach who merely turned out good, solid teams, which won three fourths of their games, looked bad by comparison.

The kind of record the Notre Dame fans yearned for was the one that Tennessee's Volunteers were making in the late thirties under General Neyland. They put three perfect seasons together in 1938, 1939, and 1940. The 1939 team was unscored upon, the last major college eleven to accomplish this almost miraculous feat. Yet Neyland did not think it was the best of the three, and all of the experts agreed with him.

The old criticism of Tennessee, that it never played the top teams from other sections, was answered in these years when the Vols went to three bowl games. The 1938 team, probably the best in the history of the school, capped its great season with a convincing 17–0 victory over Oklahoma in the Orange Bowl. Bowden Wyatt at end, the titanic guards Molinski and Suffridge, and George Cafego in the backfield were the engines that powered this perfect-record machine.

The Rose Bowl and Sugar Bowl appearances of the next two seasons, however, brought only grief. The unscored-upon team was decisively outplayed by a bigger and stronger Southern California club at Pasadena. Ambrose Schindler, a reserve tailback for the Trojans, ran through the supposedly impregnable Tennessee defense almost at will. The 14–0 final score was merciful to the Vols' reputation. They actually had been lucky that it was not twice as bad.

After the defeat there were those who said that it only proved the truth of the argument that Tennessee was unequal to the best in other areas. But losing to Southern Cal that year was no disgrace. This was one of the best Trojan teams in history, even better than the 1938 club. It was itself unbeaten, although tied by Oregon and U.C.L.A.

What Southern Cal had that Tennessee lacked was bottomless depth. Howard Jones could put three good teams on the field, and there were few opponents who could match the talent and versatility of the Trojan varsity. It was the last great eleven that Jones would coach.

Tennessee fans swallowed their disappointment and hoped for better things in the Sugar Bowl. The Vols had rolled unscathed through the 1940 season. Now they were to face the Boston College Eagles, coached by Frank Leahy, the builder of Fordham's Seven Blocks of Granite in the mid-thirties.

This was Boston College's greatest team in a long and successful football history. Its record was just as perfect as Tennessee's. In beating formidable Georgetown by a point, the Eagles had won the most exciting game ever played in Boston and ensured their supremacy in the East.

The hero of the victory, as he had been all season, was a tall, thin tailback named Charlie O'Rourke. In the final minute, with the score 19–16, he decided to run out the clock rather than punt the ball away. He galloped back and forth in his end zone, willing to give Georgetown a safety and knowing that if he dodged well enough, the time would elapse. O'Rourke was finally downed by the frantic Hoyas as mass hysteria reigned in Fenway Park, but he had won his gamble. The safety made it 19–18, and the Eagles were flying down to New Orleans to meet Tennessee on New Year's Day 1941.

The game, which observers thought certain to be dominated by defense, turned instead into a wild scoring match— at least by Tennessee standards.

Here, too, it was O'Rourke, again waiting until late in the fourth quarter, who ran for the most important touchdown in Boston College's history. To make matters worse for the crestfallen Volunteers, he used one of Neyland's favorite plays. Fading back to pass on the Tennessee 24-yard line, with the score tied 13–13, O'Rourke suddenly tucked the ball under his arm and danced past the charging defenders all the way to a touchdown. The Vols had scored dozens of times with the fake pass and run, but now they were its victims.

Leahy was hailed as one of the coming giants of his profession. But it was his last game as coach of the Eagles. Notre Dame was beckoning, and to a man who had once played for Rockne, a call from the Golden Dome was one that could not go unanswered.

Tennessee's anguish in bowl games was as nothing, however, compared to what the followers of the Duke Blue Devils of 1938 endured. Wallace Wade had created a masterpiece at Durham. Led by Eric Tipton and George McAfee, Duke went through the season unscored upon, an accomplishment that Tennessee would match the following year.

But Duke's fans argued that the 7–0 victory over Jock Sutherland's last Pitt team, in a snowstorm, showed that their heroes had played a tougher schedule than did Tennessee. Moreover, the Pitt club had its Dream Backfield, led by Marshall Goldberg, and had been beaten only by a strong Carnegie Tech eleven. Duke's triumph, ensured by its impregnable defense, made it the logical choice for a Rose Bowl bid.

Howard Jones had one of his best Southern Cal teams ready for the Blue Devils. U.S.C. won the right to go to Pasadena by stopping a rugged California team for the Bears' only defeat. Then the Trojans ended unbeaten Notre Dame's quest for a national championship. But Southern Cal had lost twice during the season to weaker opponents, and some questioned whether it could match Duke's consistency.

For fifty-eight minutes in the Rose Bowl, the answer was in doubt. Duke, playing the same defensive game it had all season long, protected a 3–0 lead with grim determination. Southern Cal began a passing attack as a last resort, with reserve quarterback Doyle Nave throwing to sophomore end Al Krueger. Down the field came the Trojans, as Duke's rapidly tiring linemen could not stop Nave's aerials, and the equally worn-out Blue Devil secondary could not cover Krueger.

Once more the great depth of the U.S.C. squad was providing the key to the Rose Bowl's outcome. With only forty seconds left and with darkness descending on the stadium, Krueger ran a clever pattern which deceived the Duke halfbacks. Nave again had time to find him as the Trojan forwards checked the defensive rush. The ball floated through the dusk and into Krueger's arms for the touchdown that gave Southern Cal its most thrilling Rose Bowl triumph and made the dispirited Duke contingent wish that the forward pass had never been legalized.

No such view prevailed in Fort Worth, Texas, that year, however. The Horned Frogs of Texas Christian University were delighted with the forward pass, and they had a right to be, for they had the aerial wizard of the season in 5'7" Davey O'Brien. With uncanny accuracy, he completed 93 out of 167 passes for 1,457 yards and 19 touchdowns. Only 4 were intercepted.

A big and good T.C.U. line, led by All-America center Ki Aldrich and tackle I. B. Hale, gave O'Brien time to find his receivers. It also made a strong running game possible, thus preventing defenses from concentrating on O'Brien. The Horned Frogs were probably the strongest team to come out of the Southwest up to that time. They were sound defensively, giving up only 53 points, while scoring 254 themselves in ten straight victories.

O'Brien was awarded the Heisman Trophy as the player of the year. In the Sugar Bowl game against Carnegie Tech, the strongest team in the East, he led T.C.U. to a 15–7 victory, completing 17 passes in 27 attempts for 225 yards and a crucial touchdown.

Tech led by a point in the third quarter, when O'Brien threw two long aerials—the last one good for 44 yards and the score—to put the Frogs back in front. Late in the game he ensured the victory with a perfect 20-yard field goal.

A huge publicity buildup had preceded the game, and the pressure on the tiny quarterback was intense, but he came through brilliantly to convince Carnegie Tech and the big crowd that he well deserved the Heisman award.

The Tartans from Pittsburgh played well and were not disgraced by losing to the team generally regarded as the best in the nation. Tech would have entered the game unbeaten if it had not been for an official's error which cost it a scoreless tie with Notre Dame. The Carnegie quarterback had asked referee John Getchell what the down was, and on being told

166

that it was third, had sent a running play into the line. Getchell, however, had made a mistake. It was in reality fourth down. He awarded the ball to Notre Dame, and the delighted Irish marched to a touchdown and a 7–0 victory.

The chagrined official won the unfortunate nickname of Wrong-Down Getchell, but when Tech went to the Sugar Bowl, it asked that he be allowed to referee the game. The mistake in downs preceded by two years the much more celebrated Red Friesell error, which immortalized the Cornell–Dartmouth meeting of 1940.

Southwestern Conference prestige reached a new national high with the great record of Texas Christian in 1938. O'Brien's aerial antics, coming as they did only two years after Sammy Baugh's, merely served to confirm the league's reputation for producing pass masters. Yet the real key to T.C.U.'s success had been its staunch defense. It seemed unlikely that the conference would see another team as sound as coach Dutch Meyer's Horned Frogs for a long time.

The very next year, however, the Texas Aggies came up with a defense that was even better and a fullback who qualified as a cowboy version of Bronko Nagurski. His name was John Kimbrough. At 6'2" and 215 pounds, he was Nagurski's size, and he was equally devastating as a line plunger. The Aggie defense, led by guard Marshall Foch Robnett, limited ten regular-season opponents to a pair of touchdowns, a field goal, and a safety. Coach Homer Norton employed a double wingback offense, which made full use of Kimbrough's ability to run around the ends as well as through the middle. There was little attempt at razzle-dazzle.

Oddly enough, however, it was a rare deceptive maneuver which brought victory against unbeaten Tulane in the Sugar Bowl and preserved Texas A. & M.'s number one national rating. Trailing 13–7, quarterback Walemon Price completed a seemingly routine pass to end Herb Smith, who then pitched a perfect lateral to Kimbrough. The big fullback ran over a pair of Tulane tacklers and scored the touchdown that tied the game. Price kicked the extra point, and the Aggies had their perfect season.

With Kimbrough carrying the burden of the offense,

the Aggies went on winning in 1940. They remained a difficult team to score upon, since Kimbrough was as good at backing up a line as he was at shattering one when he had the ball. In addition, as with any really good team, there were a dozen other excellent players to perform the blocking and tackling necessities. As the Aggies came down to their final game, all they needed was a victory over Texas to finish a second perfect season.

Dana X. Bible had been rebuilding the broken football machine at Austin, and his efforts were now showing results. The Longhorns, although twice beaten, had won six games and were playing well defensively. Their strategy against the Aggies was to strike quickly for a touchdown and then contain Kimbrough on the ground.

In the opening moments Texas quarterback Pete Layden threw a long pass to Noble Doss for a touchdown. Texas A. & M. was stunned, and for the rest of the afternoon a tenacious Longhorn defense never let the Aggies regain their momentum. The 7–0 upset was one of the highlights of Texas' football history. The Aggies, however, were still the conference champion and went to the Cotton Bowl to play Fordham.

Sleepy Jim Crowley had finally found the breakaway runners he had always needed to make his Rose Hill Rams go on offense. Fordham was traditionally strong defensively, but the lack of a long-distance threat on the ground had greatly reduced its scoring potential. Now, however, Crowley had Len Eshmont and Jim Blumenstock at the halfbacks, and Fordham began making touchdowns as never before. When they reached the Cotton Bowl, the Rams owned a perfect record.

They outplayed the Aggies decisively, holding them to 52 yards on the ground, but were the victims of a sleeper play and a key penalty, which combined to give Texas A. & M. a 13–12 victory. Fordham's chance to tie the score late in the game was foiled when its second extra-point attempt was blocked. Thus the Aggies won another bowl game by a single point.

Dana Bible's Texas Longhorns took the center of the stage in 1941 with the highest-scoring team the Southwest

Conference had yet seen. Six straight opponents were man-handled as the furious Texas touchdown machine averaged more than 40 points per game. Lowly Baylor was not expected to provide anything more than token opposition for the team that was riding atop the wire-service rankings.

The Bears from Waco had absorbed four consecutive defeats, including an awesome 48–0 drubbing from Texas A. & M. But somehow an indefinable mixture of Baylor pride and Texas overconfidence combined to produce the surprise of the year, a 7–7 tie. The Longhorns were so crestfallen that they failed to meet the challenge of their ancient jinx, Texas Christian, the following week, and the Horned Frogs handed them a one-touchdown defeat.

All that remained for Bible's shattered legions was the chance to spoil Texas A. & M.'s perfect season, as they had done the year before. This time the Longhorns played up to their full potential and swept the Aggies off the field by an amazing score of 23–0.

But if that was decisive, it was nothing compared to what Texas did to Oregon a week later. The Ducks were by no means a great team, but they had played a close game with Rose Bowl-bound Oregon State, their arch intrastate rival. Against Texas, however, they were destroyed 71–7.

It had been a season of deep frustration for Bible's club, despite the fact that it had won eight out of ten games. Texas partisans, and many observers in other parts of the country as well, felt that the Longhorns had the best personnel of any team. Yet Minnesota, Duke, and Notre Dame, all undefeated, had finished higher in the wire-service ratings.

Minnesota, on the way to its second straight national title, had been able to win the big games and had not been victimized by overconfidence. Long after the season ended, Texas fans still found it hard to believe that their team had been tied by Baylor. And even in Waco it still seemed a dream.

19. Return of the T

Twelve years after Pop Warner had astonished the East with his new double wingback formation, another Stanford coach was getting ready to change the entire offensive structure of the game. He was Clark Daniel Shaughnessy, newly arrived in Palo Alto from the University of Chicago, where he had served as that school's second, and last, football coach. The university had abandoned the sport, and Stagg Field was now turned over to a group of physicists headed by Enrico Fermi for endeavors far more destructive than mere blocking and tackling.

Shaughnessy's seven years on the Midway produced no formidable teams. But one supremely gifted player, Jay Berwanger, did give the suffering Maroon fans something to cheer about. Berwanger was the first winner of the Heisman Trophy. He was adept at every aspect of the game, but especially outstanding as a running back. Had he played on a team with better blockers, Berwanger might have broken every record in the book.

When Shaughnessy arrived in Palo Alto, he could have used a Berwanger. Stanford had fallen on hard times, and the alumni were calling for either a swift improvement or the coach's contract. The Indians had been using the time-honored single and double wingback formations, but the personnel seemed all wrong.

With necessity helping the inventive process, Shaughnessy began tinkering with a new formation. It was, in reality, an old formation, the oldest in the game. He took the basic

170

T alignment—in which the quarterback crouches behind the center and the other backs form a line a few yards to the rear—and added a few refinements. He put one of the halfbacks in motion, thus opening up a host of new pass patterns and forcing the defense to compensate accordingly. He then plotted a series of exchanges in which the quarterback would whirl and hand the ball quickly to a charging fullback or halfback.

Each maneuver had variations with multiple options, and the plays were to be run at top speed. The linemen were merely to bump the defense off balance and then rush downfield to block the secondary. The double-team blocking, which distinguished the wingback formations, was not necessary. The emphasis was all on the quick opening play in which a fast halfback would dart through the line before the defense could adjust.

What this formation needed more than anything else was a quarterback who could both handle the ball with great dexterity and pass with accuracy. He need not be a runner, and he would be far too valuable to risk as a blocker. Thus the runner-passer, which the single wing must have to be successful, was not essential in Shaughnessy's new T formation. He was unusually fortunate to find on the Stanford varsity an ineffective double wing tailback who would become not only the first of the modern T formation quarterbacks but one of the best of them all. His name was Frank Albert.

As if by providence, there were other players on the squad who would also fit perfectly into Shaughnessy's new scheme. There were two halfbacks, Pete Kmetovic and Hugh Gallarneau, who had the requisite speed and blocking ability. And there was a big, mobile fullback, Norman Standlee, who could both hit the line and protect the passer. The four combined to become the greatest backfield in Stanford's history.

The team which had been the laughing stock of the Coast in 1939 became the most exciting club in football a year later. The Indians began winning games in September and rolled through nine straight for a perfect season. They did

not run up huge scores, and their defense, while adequate, was not nearly as good as that of the Vow Boys. But when it came time to name a host for the Rose Bowl, there could be no other selection. Shaughnessy's Indians were pitted against a powerful Nebraska team, which had swept through the midlands, losing only to the eventual national champion, Minnesota.

The game turned into a showcase for the modern T formation. Albert's brilliant faking mystified the big Cornhusker linemen, and the quick opening thrusts of Kmetovic and Gallarneau gained consistently. But Nebraska was a formidable team too. It moved out to a 7–0 lead, as single wing power plays pushed Stanford back. Then the Indians marched down the field on T-formation runs and passes. With the ball at the Nebraska 9-yard line, Albert cleverly handed it to Gallarneau and faked so convincingly that the big halfback had scored before the defense realized he was the carrier. Later in the game, after Nebraska had scored again, Albert threw a long pass to Gallarneau for another touchdown. And to ensure the victory, Kmetovic returned a punt for a third score.

The hundreds of coaches who watched the game were profoundly impressed by Stanford's offensive capability. What made it all the more meaningful was the fact that Nebraska was such a strong defensive team. If the T formation worked so well against an eleven as good as the Cornhuskers, the coaches reasoned, it must indeed be the wave of the future.

The parallel success of the Chicago Bears in winning the professional championship from the Washington Redskins by an unbelievable 73–0 score only served to emphasize the impact of the new formation. Shaughnessy had taught the T to the Bears too. He was now the most influential coach in all of football.

Stanford's victory was the fourth in succession for a Pacific champion in the Rose Bowl. Southern Cal had won twice over unscored-upon Southern teams, and the year before that, California had handed Alabama its first bowl defeat.

The Golden Bears of 1937 were one of the finest squads in West Coast history. They were as good as the best of the

Frankie Albert of Stanford, first of   173
the modern T-formation quarterbacks.
Famous at the tender age of twenty-one,
but the helmet still fit.

California Wonder Teams of fifteen years earlier. Sportswriters began calling the Bears the Thunder Team. They had five All-America players in the lineup: Perry Schwartz at end, Vard Stockton at guard, Bob Herwig at center, and Sam Chapman and Vic Bottari in the backfield. Only Washington succeeded in containing them during the regular season in a 0–0 tie. Nine other opponents were soundly defeated.

The Alabama team that came to play these rugged Californians at Pasadena had a perfect record, but it had been fortunate to win two big games on field goals.

In the Rose Bowl it was all California, as the big Bear line tackled and blocked so fiercely that Alabama never had a chance. The final score was 13–0, with the running of Bottari accounting for both touchdowns. The Alabama contingent agreed sadly that the score could have been two or three times worse, so completely was the Crimson Tide outplayed.

The decisiveness of California's victory caused a bitter argument over which team, the Bears, Pitt, or Fordham, deserved the national championship. The Associated Press poll named the Panthers, but those who saw the Rose Bowl game could not imagine a better eleven than California's Thunder Team.

Three undefeated and untied Southern teams had come to grief at Pasadena in four years. Duke and Tennessee, both unscored upon, followed Alabama in defeat, and each time, the West Coast team that won the game had lacked a perfect record.

As the 1941 season reached its conclusion, it became apparent that Duke had turned out perhaps its greatest team. The Blue Devils were rated second only to Minnesota in the national polls. They had won nine straight and scored 311 points, a much better offensive showing than their 1938 team had made. They were good on defense too, but could not quite equal the unscored-upon mark of the 1938 club.

Duke fans wanted a Rose Bowl triumph more than anything else. They had never fully recovered from the last-second defeat by Southern California and were certain that this time they had the offense to win at Pasadena. When the

174

Duke camp learned that its opponent on New Year's Day would be Oregon State, its confidence reached a new high. The Beavers had been beaten twice, and some observers went so far as to suggest that the game would be a mismatch. But what was being overlooked was the fact that State had gathered momentum at midseason and was a first-rate team when it won the bowl nomination.

The usual preparations were under way at Pasadena when the world outside the gridiron cruelly intervened. The Japanese bombed Pearl Harbor and the West Coast became a potential war zone. All large gatherings were prohibited. It seemed as though the Rose Bowl had been an early casualty of the war, but the game's sponsors took one last chance to save it. They accepted the generous offer of Duke's coach Wallace Wade to move the festivities to Durham.

Oregon State made the cross-country trek to this most improbable of Rose Bowl sites and proceeded to play the heavily favored Blue Devils on even terms into the third period. State was led by Don Durden, who scored one touchdown and passed for another. Duke relied on its All-America halfback Steve Lach. It was 14–14 when the Beavers took the ball at their own 32-yard line.

Here quarterback Bob Dethman faded back and arched a long spiral to reserve halfback Gene Gray. The fast-moving State receiver caught the ball on the Duke 28 and ran the remaining distance for the touchdown that gave his school the greatest victory in its history. The final score was Oregon State 20, Duke 16.

For the Blue Devils it was another heartbreaking defeat in the Rose Bowl, although this time they had at least the consolation of being spared the long ride home.

20. A Halfback Named Harmon

Fritz Crisler was always a man to rise to a challenge, and in the autumn of 1938 he was faced with a big one: get Michigan back on the winning track. The Wolverines, after four wildly successful seasons in the early thirties, had staggered through defeat after defeat. The "punt, pass, and prayer" philosophy seemed hopelessly outdated, or perhaps it was just that the material which had made the system work so well was no longer there.

Whatever the cause, the proud old giant of Midwestern football was wallowing in despair. Its far-flung and zealous alumni leaped to the barricades, however, and did what far-flung and zealous alumni always do in a situation such as this. They went out looking for large and swift academicians. The athletic department did its part by luring Crisler from Princeton with the promise that he would find a new phalanx of talented players awaiting him.

This turned out to be a considerable understatement. When Crisler looked at his sophomore-dominated varsity in September of 1938, he saw one youngster who was a phalanx all by himself. He was Tom Harmon of Gary, Indiana, the most sought-after high school star in the nation, and he was destined to live up to all of his advance billing and then some. Harmon was ably supported by a number of other gifted athletes, the best known of whom was Forest Evashevski, who blocked for him, called the plays, and for three years was Michigan's leader on the field. Such All-America linemen as Ralph Heikkinen, Ed Frutig, Albert Wistert, and Bob Ingalls

176

formed the backbone of the Harmon teams of 1938–39–40.

From their first game, in which they ended Michigan State's four-year domination of the Wolverines, it was evident that Crisler's men would restore the lost prestige. Only one defeat was sustained in 1938, and that by a single point at the hands of Big Ten champion Minnesota.

The next year Crisler found the perfect spinning fullback to crack the line and handle the ball, an essential in his deceptive single wing offense. He was Bob Westfall, a small but sturdy hometown boy from Ann Arbor. With Evashevski, Harmon, and Paul Kromer, Westfall joined to form one of the best backfields in Michigan's history. They began 1939 in high style by winning their first four games in convincing fashion. One was an 85–0 victory over Crisler's alma mater, the University of Chicago.

It had been on the Midway one afternoon more than twenty years before that Crisler first met the man who was to change his life. Amos Alonzo Stagg was running along the sideline watching his Maroons scrimmage when he was abruptly knocked down by a freshman who somehow got in his way. Stagg told the frightened youth to put on a football uniform if he liked doing that sort of thing, and Fritz Crisler obeyed. Despite the fact that he had not played in high school, Crisler made the varsity as a lightweight end. By the time he was a senior, he was good enough to win a place on Walter Camp's second-team All-America. Crisler did brilliantly in the classroom and seemed headed for a medical career when Stagg chose him as an assistant.

Once he got into the routine of coaching, Crisler's unfettered imagination made him a wizard at devising offensive maneuvers. His Princeton teams bewildered their opponents, and at Michigan his single wing seemed equally to arise from a bottomless bag of tricks. By the time the Wolverines rolled into Champaign, they were the talk of the country, and the experts were comparing Harmon to Red Grange. Some were even saying that he was better.

Bob Zuppke carefully collected these appraisals and fed them to his undernourished Illinois players. They then went out and ruined Michigan, 16–7, in the upset of the year.

The Illini had a way of destroying other teams' perfect seasons, and of all their victims Michigan was the favorite. The Wolverines were so disoriented that they failed to find their way against Minnesota the following week and were upset again.

With the season in a shambles, they rose up at the end and struck down Ohio State's conference champions, as little Fred Trosko scored the winning touchdown on a fake field goal, one of Fielding Yost's original inventions from years before.

The past disappointments were forgotten as Michigan opened its 1940 season. Harmon and Evashevski were now seniors, as were many of the top linemen. Harmon had made the 1939 All-America team at halfback, and even bigger things were expected of him.

It would be hard to top his performance against Pennsylvania at Franklin Field, however. In that game, which Michigan won by 2 points, the great tailback had gone back to pass, run from sideline to sideline, retreated 30 yards, and then turned and raced down the field to a touchdown. He covered something like 140 yards in all, and even years later, when the film was shown again and again, it still seemed an utterly impossible journey.

Harmon gave notice in his first game of 1940 that he would be every bit as good. He ran wild against California at Berkeley, scoring on runs of 94 and 75 yards before the dumbfounded Bears knew what had happened. He was just as good against Harvard, and in the encounter with an unbeaten Pennsylvania team, he outperformed Francis X. Reagan to lead Michigan to a 14–0 victory.

Harmon was the perfect single wing tailback. At 6'1" and 193 pounds, he had the size to run the vital off-tackle cutback. He was fast and elusive in the open field, possessing that often-described sixth sense which is attributed to game-breaking runners. All of the great ones have it, and yet no coach can claim credit. The talent seems to be inborn.

What made Harmon even more formidable was his passing ability. He would have been a sensation merely as a running back, but with his aerial accomplishments added, he was a

Tom Harmon, "Old Number 98" of Michigan. There were ten other Wolverines on the team, but nobody seemed to notice.

once-in-a-generation superstar. He also punted, place-kicked, and played defense, but no one seemed to notice, so astonishing were his offensive skills. He was the only modern Big Ten back who could be mentioned with Red Grange—and to Michigan's followers, at least, Harmon's name came first.

Evashevski played a role in Harmon's career similar to the one which Earl Britton occupied in Grange's. The big quarterback was the premier blocker of his time, and no one appreciated his manifold talents more than did Harmon.

For these two and their teammates the game with Minnesota was the crucial test of the season. When they arrived at Minneapolis, rain accompanied them, turning the field into a mire that would favor the bigger, slower Gophers. Michigan's precisely geared offense needed a dry field, and the only advantage her smaller line had would be the sure footing that would enable it to use its speed.

But the Gophers did not need to rely on mud to cope with Michigan. They were an exceedingly formidable team themselves, with a power-oriented offense. If they could not match Michigan's speed and passing, they were unquestionably superior in short-yardage situations and on defense.

Both squads were well-endowed with present and future All-America nominees. Michigan had Frutig, Wistert, Ingalls, Harmon, and Westfall, and there were many who would have included Evashevski as well. Minnesota had its two great tackles, Wildung and Odson, Helge Pukema at guard, Bill Daley at fullback, and two sparkling halfbacks, George Franck and Bruce Smith. Franck was named to the All-America backfield with Harmon. Smith was the Heisman Trophy winner the following year.

Michigan disregarded the field conditions and moved for a touchdown with Harmon passing to Evashevski, but the former's extra-point effort went awry. Shortly after the score, the Wolverines blocked a Minnesota punt and were on the verge of a second touchdown.

The Gophers, knowing that a two-touchdown deficit against such a strong opponent would be fatal, braced and contained Michigan. On the first play after it regained the ball, Minnesota sent Smith through left tackle for 80 yards and a touchdown. A reserve halfback named Joe Mernik kicked the extra point, and the first half ended with the home team ahead 7–6.

The final thirty minutes saw Michigan threaten often but never score, as the desperate Gopher defense preserved its 1-point advantage. Minnesota was to win both the Big Ten and national championships on the strength of its successful conversion. Michigan fans went away muttering about a different outcome on a dry field, but all were agreed that these were indeed two of the best teams of the entire decade.

In the Northwestern game a week later, Michigan met a team which had lost only once, to Minnesota, and also by a single point. Harmon made the big play in the final quarter to give the Wolverines a 20–13 victory over one of the Purple's strongest elevens.

There now remained only the season's finale against traditional rival Ohio State at Columbus. The Buckeyes had played Minnesota a close game, losing by a 13–7 score, and expected to do well against Harmon. But the nation's leading player reached his peak, along with the rest of the Michigan team, and Ohio State was buried 40–0 for its worst defeat since joining the Big Ten.

Harmon won every award in sight, including the Heisman Trophy. He led the country in scoring, with 117 points. He had also finished first in 1939, with 112. In the years since, no player has won the scoring title more than once. Harmon ran for nearly 900 yards and passed for 500 more in his senior year. In three seasons he scored 237 points, more even than the fabled Red Grange.

The only other Midwestern back who dominated his team's offense to a comparable degree during this time was Nile Kinnick of Iowa. He was every bit as versatile as Harmon, but the Hawkeye teams on which he played lacked Michigan's overall depth and talent.

Kinnick reached his peak in 1939, when he and the Iowa Iron Men played practically sixty-minute football throughout a grueling campaign. They registered thrilling victories over Notre Dame and Minnesota on successive Saturdays. The Gophers were beaten in a furious last-quarter rally in which

Kinnick played the decisive role. The only team to throttle them was Harmon's Michigan, and it took one of the Wolverine star's greatest performances to do it.

Kinnick gave Iowa a taste of the glory which had been absent for nearly a generation, since the days of the Devine team of the early twenties. He was a strong but not a great runner, a deadly accurate passer, a consistent punter and extrapoint kicker, and a sure-handed receiver of punts and kickoffs. He called all of Iowa's plays and was the inspirational leader of the team as well.

In his senior year Kinnick had a hand in nearly every touchdown the Hawkeyes made. He scored five himself and passed for eleven more, in addition to playing flawlessly on defense. He was as close to being a complete football player as any man who has ever stepped on a gridiron.

Kinnick was the Heisman Trophy winner in 1939. He also managed to pick up a Phi Beta Kappa key for his work in the classroom, and planned to follow a career in the law. But Pearl Harbor intervened, and he entered the Naval Air Corps instead. On June 2, 1943, Nile Kinnick died when his plane crashed in the Gulf of Paria off the coast of Venezuela.

Nile Kinnick of Iowa. Hawkeye immortal,
and the complete football player.

21. Brave Old Army Team

The war did strange things to football. It wiped out the sport entirely at some schools. At others it brought in players from rival institutions, creating, in effect, virtual all-star teams.

The service academies, West Point and Annapolis, became magnets for some of the finest athletes in the country. Army, in particular, had the strongest elevens in its history, completely dominating the game in 1944 and 1945. It took a few years, however, for the influx of talent to assert itself. In 1942 and 1943 West Point was badly outplayed by Notre Dame. It seemed an incongruity that the Army was being asked to defeat both the Germans and the Japanese when it could not seem to cope with the Irish.

But by 1944 Colonel Earl Blaik had welcomed such stalwarts as John Green, Barney Poole, and Joe Stanowicz in the line, and Doug Kenna, Glenn Davis, and Felix "Doc" Blanchard in the backfield. They were soon joined by end Hank Foldberg and tackles DeWitt "Tex" Coulter and Al Nemetz. More backfield aces descended upon the plains above the Hudson. Max Minor came from Texas, Tom McWilliams from Mississippi State, and Arnold Tucker from Miami. Dick Walterhouse arrived from Ann Arbor to kick the extra points and, as it turned out, he was to have many opportunities. These men joined with experienced regulars Tom Lombardo and Dale Hall (later West Point's coach) to give Army more backfield depth than any team had ever known.

The Cadets went swiftly through their 1944 schedule, scoring 504 points to 35. Notre Dame's depleted wartime team was destroyed 59–0, the worst defeat in the school's history. Army rooters called for still more touchdowns, thus angering many of Notre Dame's New York "subway alumni," who felt that the military was engaging in war crimes against defenseless civilians. It was true that the Black Knights were pouring it on. They had suffered nothing but defeat at Notre Dame's hands for nearly a generation, and now they were assuaging their frustrations with a vengeance.

Only once all season was Army given a real test. The landslide victories over civilian schools were suspect because of the dearth of material on the home front. But Navy was thought to be almost the Cadets' equal. The Middies had transfers from other schools, too. Don Whitmire, from Alabama, an All-America tackle, was in the line along with Dick Duden and Ben Chase. The backfield, with Bob Jenkins and Clyde "Smackover" Scott, was also deep in talent. It was a close game for three quarters, but Davis broke it up with a long run and the Army won 23–7.

The next season was practically a repeat performance, with the Cadets rolling up 412 points. Again Notre Dame was slaughtered, this time 48–0, as the fires of outrage burned ever higher in South Bend.

Michigan turned in one of the surprises of the year by playing the Black Knights on even terms for three periods. Fritz Crisler came up with the novel idea of substituting entire units in an effort to spare his seventeen-year-old freshmen the full brunt of the Army attack. The bigger Michigan players were used on defense, while the smaller, faster men tried to move the ball. Although the Cadets finally pushed across three touchdowns late in the game to win 28–7, the Wolverines won considerable praise for their stout performance, and Crisler's platooning innovation made a profound impression upon his fellow coaches.

It had actually been an idea derived from Knute Rockne's days at Notre Dame. The Irish in the twenties used a special second string called shock troops, whose function it was to wear down the other team during the first quarter. Then

Rockne would insert his regulars, and they would run all over their tired opponents. In those days, players stayed in the game on both offense and defense. Crisler merely modified the concept to add the element of specialization.

After the war, when hordes of experienced players returned to the campuses, many schools took up platooning, with Michigan, Notre Dame, and Army enjoying perhaps the greatest success. The free-substitution rule has gone through a series of modifications, with periodic attempts being made to outlaw platooning. But the trend has been clearly in the direction of separate units for offense and defense.

When Army and Navy met at the end of the 1945 season, it marked the first time that they had both brought undefeated records into the game. Navy had been tied by Notre Dame, but still was thought to have its best team since the 1926 national champions of Frank Wickhorst and Tom Hamilton. Army, however, was still a better club, and won a tense duel 32–13.

Blanchard, who possessed unusual speed for a fullback, was the key to the Cadet attack, as he had been all season. He enjoyed a remarkable 7-yard average gain every time he carried the ball. Since the majority of his running had been through the most densely packed sector of the line, this achievement was even more astonishing.

Davis averaged better than 11 yards per play in both 1944 and 1945. He was a blazingly fast open-field runner with a change of pace that made him practically impossible to contain. He crossed enemy goal lines fifty-nine times in his career, the most prolific touchdown maker since Willie Heston.

A team which had either Blanchard or Davis in its backfield would present serious problems for any defense. With both, Army possessed probably the most devastating rushing combination of all time. At 6'1" and 205 pounds, Blanchard had the size to hammer the line and fit his "Mr. Inside" nickname. Davis was 5'9" and 170 pounds, and could run 100 yards in 9.7 seconds. He was thus the perfect "Mr. Outside" to go with Blanchard. An excellent but inevitably

Mr. Outside. Glenn Davis of Army
in full stride.

less heralded quarterback, Arnold Tucker, adroitly directed their sorties.

It was not until 1946, however, that Army really proved itself to be a great team. Ironically, it lost the mythical national title that year to Notre Dame. The ex-servicemen came back to all the schools on the Army schedule, and the easy Saturdays of the past two seasons were replaced by grueling encounters with some of the strongest teams in the country.

Oklahoma gave the Cadets a difficult time in their opening game before losing by a pair of touchdowns. Two weeks later, in Ann Arbor, the Army had to rally in the last quarter to beat Michigan 20–13. It was one of the most thrilling games on record, as the Wolverines, only a year away from all-time greatness, baffled the Cadets with their intricate offense.

Davis saved the game with a desperation pass that was caught by end Bob Folsom for a touchdown. It had appeared to be a broken play, with the ball bounding crazily through the Army backfield. As the Wolverines charged in to recover the fumble, Davis scooped up the ball and threw it, all in a single motion, in the general direction of the end zone. The touchdown sent Army into a 13–7 halftime lead.

When Michigan later tied the score with a long, brilliant march, Davis regained the initiative for his team with consistent running and passing. Blanchard finally scored the winning touchdown on a short plunge, and when the Wolverines threatened in the closing moments, Davis once again rose to the occasion with an interception at the goal line.

As exciting as this game was, however, the one that every football fan awaited was the meeting with Notre Dame at the Yankee Stadium. The Battle of the Century they were calling it. The Irish had welcomed back dozens of first-rate players, including the greatest tackle in the school's history, George Connor, guard John Mastrangelo, center George Strohmeyer, and quarterback Johnny Lujack.

Notre Dame had defeated Big Ten champion Illinois, then breezed past Pittsburgh, Purdue, Iowa, and Navy. It had what may have been the strongest Irish defense in history.

Mr. Inside. Army's Doc Blanchard being urged to stop by a crowd of tired Pennsylvanians.

Coach Frank Leahy, back after two years in the Navy, had a productive offense to go with it, and until the Army game, his team had not even been tested, much less extended.

Those who saw the contest as a meeting of the irresistible force and the immovable object were proven exactly correct. Before a spellbound audience of 70,000, the two juggernauts ground to a screeching 0–0 halt. So well-matched were they that the statistics were all but identical. There was a moment when Blanchard appeared to be loose in the open field, but along came the indomitable Lujack to make a sure and crucial tackle. Likewise, when the Irish threatened, the Army manned its barricade and hurled the Midwesterners back.

Both coaches were accused of undue conservatism, but their reluctance to risk defeat was more than understandable. These were obviously the two best teams of the year, and many thought that they should be named co-champions in the Associated Press poll.

Things might have worked out that way had not a determined Navy eleven played with such inspiration that the Cadets were given their biggest scare of the season. Army jumped out to a convincing two-touchdown lead and appeared headed for an easy victory. But the Midshipmen put on a furious last-quarter rally that narrowed the score to 21–18. With time running out, they got the ball near the Army goal line and were frantically trying for the touchdown that would have given them the greatest upset in the history of football. The clock thwarted the Navy, however, and Army's undefeated team left the field shaken but triumphant.

It had been such a decided moral victory for the Middies that the Associated Press poll relegated Army to second place behind Notre Dame. The Helms Foundation, however, insisted that the Cadets were number one.

Although most experts agreed with the Associated Press, Blaik and his players still were jubilant, for they were celebrating that rarest of football accomplishments: three successive undefeated seasons. Blanchard and Davis were the most renowned West Point heroes since Chris Cagle and All-America center Edgar Garbisch, whose four field goals had beaten the Navy 12–0 a generation before.

190

Colonel Earl H. "Red" Blaik and his troops in 1945. From left, Doc Blanchard, Glenn Davis, Blaik, Tom McWilliams, and Arnold Tucker. The civilians got zapped, and the Navy did too.

Yet there were some critics who suggested that it had taken the catastrophe of the war to bring these outstanding athletes to West Point, and that in normal times, whatever they were, neither Blaik nor Army football would have enjoyed such status. It took precisely two seasons for the taciturn Colonel to prove them all wrong. But when his true coaching genius finally had been hailed on all sides, he then had to conquer a profound personal misfortune.

22. The War Years

At some universities football not only survived during the war years but reached its highest level. In 1942 Georgia turned out its finest team up to that time. Wisconsin and Ohio State fielded powerful squads, with the Buckeyes winning the national championship under the cool and calculating direction of Paul Brown.

Frank Leahy's Notre Dame eleven of 1943 was far and away the best in the nation, despite a last-second defeat by the Great Lakes Naval Training Station. The sailors were loaded with big-name college players, and it was Duke's All-America halfback Steve Lach who threw the touchdown pass that ruined the Irish, 19–14. Notre Dame had beaten Northwestern, Michigan, Navy, Army, and the star-studded Iowa Naval Pre-Flight School, coached by Bernie Bierman.

The core of the offense was an uncanny passer named Angelo Bertelli, who earned the sobriquet the Springfield Rifle both for his ability to throw a football on target and in deference to his hometown in Massachusetts. Creighton Miller, son of a famous Notre Dame halfback of the pre-Rockne era, was the season's premier broken-field runner. Many South Bend observers rate him as the best in the history of the school. Bertelli won the 1943 Heisman Trophy and joined Miller in the All-America backfield.

Alabama also returned to championship form during the war years, with a passer who was literally ten feet tall. Harry Gilmer, an eighteen-year-old sensation in 1945, would take the ball from center Vaughn Mancha and fade back to throw.

Angelo Bertelli of Notre Dame. The Heisman Trophy winner in 1943 about to launch one of his perfectly aimed aerials.

The 5'10" Gilmer would then leap high into the air, spot his receiver downfield, and fling the ball with phenomenal accuracy. He led the Crimson Tide to a perfect season, capped by a 34–14 rout of Southern California in the Rose Bowl, the first loss at Pasadena for the Trojans.

Alabama was in need of a Gilmer in its backfield that day in 1942 when it succumbed to the Georgia team led by "Fireball" Frankie Sinkwich. The score stood 10–0 in the Tide's favor as the fourth quarter began, but Georgia put on a three-touchdown finish to win the game. Several weeks later, an undefeated Georgia Tech team was routed by Sinkwich, his backfield partner, Charlie Trippi, and the horde of able players coached by Wallace Butts.

Sinkwich played despite a broken jaw, and was fitted with a protective device which caused him to be called the Man in the Iron Mask. It reminded historians of the same nickname which had been applied to the great Jay Berwanger at the University of Chicago seven years earlier. The mask did not restrict Sinkwich's activities, however, as the Youngstown, Ohio, triple threat ran and passed for more than 2,400 yards.

Sinkwich was a unanimous All-America selection and the winner of the Heisman Trophy. The only honor left for him was to lead Georgia to victory in the Rose Bowl, but he suffered an ankle injury and had to sit out most of the game. Trippi, however, filled in admirably as Georgia outplayed U.C.L.A. to win 9–0.

Wisconsin and Ohio State met in the biggest game of the 1942 season, and the Badgers won by 10 points with their best team in more than a generation. It was led by All-America end Dave Schreiner, fullback Pat Harder, and the elusive Elroy "Crazylegs" Hirsch. Ohio State recovered from the setback and won the rest of its games, but Wisconsin could not stand prosperity, and fell victim to the year's most startling upset, a 6–0 loss to Iowa.

Paul Brown, the most successful high school coach in the country, had come from Massillon to Columbus to get the Buckeyes back on the winning habit. In his first year he

194   *Otto Graham, Northwestern's triple-threat single
                   wing tailback, carries the ball around
             Michigan at Ann Arbor in 1941. Nice try, Otto,
                but the Wolverines won 14–7. Number 11
                        for Michigan is Albert Wistert.*

lost only to Northwestern, which had Otto Graham at the top of his form, and managed to tie Michigan. In 1942 the Buckeyes beat both.

Two years later they triumphed again with a team led by Heisman Trophy winner Les Horvath, end Jack Dugger, tackle Bill Willis, and guard Bill Hackett. Horvath was not especially big or fast, but he had an unexcelled strategic intelligence, was a proficient all-round player, and held a sophomore-dominated team together.

No one expected the Buckeyes to win the Big Ten championship, but they did just that, and won all their games in the process. The opposition wilted for eight straight weeks, but in the traditional finale with Michigan the outcome was in doubt until the last minute. Horvath led a 50-yard march after a short kickoff by the Wolverines, and Ohio State won an 18–14 thriller that gave it a perfect season. Paul Brown had left to direct the Great Lakes team, turning things over to his chief assistant, Carroll Widdoes. Thus the new coach achieved an all-victorious record in his first season.

The war years also brought Indiana its first Big Ten championship and an undefeated team in 1945. Coached by the old Centre College quarterback, Bo McMillin, the Hoosiers combined a stout defense with the point-scoring heroics of Pete Pihos and sophomore tailback George Taliaferro to win nine games.

Indiana had unusual pride and the strong motivation that comes to a team when it knows that it is accomplishing something that has never been done before. Always the doormat of the rugged conference, this time the squad McMillin jestingly called his "poor li'l boys" turned out to be anything but that.

23. The Man from Winner

Frank Leahy spent his boyhood in the prophetically named town of Winner, South Dakota. He went to Notre Dame in the late twenties to play tackle for Rockne, but a knee injury ended his career. It turned out, however, to be a landmark in Leahy's life, comparable to Fritz Crisler's collision with Alonzo Stagg on the Midway. Leahy was given the privilege of attending every Notre Dame practice and of sitting in on all of the coaching sessions. This was equivalent to a seminar in the fine points of the game, and the eager youngster took full advantage of it. Later he shared a hospital room with Rockne when the coach went to the Mayo Clinic for treatment of a blood clot. Leahy was admitted for knee surgery but seemed almost unaware of his ailment, so mesmerized was he by Rockne's discourses on football.

When Leahy left the Golden Dome, he went first to Georgetown, then to Michigan State to assist Jim Crowley. The two quickly moved to Fordham, where each won considerable acclaim, Leahy serving as line coach of the famed Seven Blocks of Granite. It was no surprise then that Boston College should lure him to Chestnut Hill to get the Eagles airborne once again. This Leahy did, turning out the best team in the school's history in 1940. There was now only one place to go, and Leahy went there the next year.

Notre Dame responded to its new coach by going undefeated, although tied by Army, in 1941. Not since Rockne's 1930 national champions had the Irish achieved an unbeaten record. Leahy was named coach of the year in his first season

197

at South Bend. The next campaign saw defeats by Georgia Tech and Michigan, as Crisler's Wolverines broke open a close game with a three-touchdown explosion in the second half.

In 1943, however, the Irish climbed to the top of the heap by defeating all possible civilian rivals. A last-second letdown against the Great Lakes Naval Training Center ruined the perfect season, but not the number one rating. A satisfied Leahy then went into the Navy for two seasons while Notre Dame did its part in the war effort by serving as cannon fodder for Red Blaik's Army teams.

Leahy knew that he would have an unusually strong varsity when he returned to the campus in 1946, but it is doubtful if even he realized just how overwhelming Notre Dame would be.

Johnny Lujack was the key to the success of the 1946 and 1947 squads. He was a competent passer, a good runner, and a full-fledged wizard at ball handling and play calling. He was also a commanding personality whose presence in the lineup was the equivalent of having a coach on the field. But the one particular talent which surpassed even these remarkable gifts was Lujack's unmatched capability on defense. He was the best in the country at it, with such an uncanny knack for diagnosing the other side's plays that it almost seemed as though he could read the opposing quarterback's mind.

Lujack had some of the finest players in Notre Dame's history to help him with his heroics. Leon Hart and Jim Martin at ends, Zygmont Czarobski at tackle, Bill Fischer at guard, and Terry Brennan and Emil Sitko in the backfield joined with the stars of the 1946 team to make 1947 an even better year for the Irish. They raced through to a perfect record, with Brennan sealing the Army's doom on the opening kickoff by returning it 97 yards to a touchdown. It was Earl Blaik's last chance to beat a Leahy-coached Notre Dame team, but the Cadets, without Blanchard and Davis, were unequal to the challenge and lost by three touchdowns. Thus Blaik, in five meetings with Leahy, had to be content with a pair of scoreless ties and three defeats.

Johnny Lujack of Notre Dame. Just like having a coach on the field.

Notre Dame had trouble only with Northwestern in 1947, finally outlasting the fired-up Wildcats by 7 points. After the season's concluding game, in which a strong U.S.C. team was beaten 38–7, the Associated Press poll awarded the national championship to the Irish, over the outraged protests of Michigan's partisans.

When Lujack graduated, it was thought that perhaps Notre Dame might now be vulnerable at quarterback, but Frank Tripuka filled in admirably in 1948, and the horde of big, mobile linemen and hard-running backs continued to overpower the opposition.

The team scored more points than either of its undefeated predecessors, but it was not as good on defense, and this nearly cost it three games. Purdue was defeated 28–27 in a wild opener which left both sides exhausted. The Boilermakers had to play their two most difficult Big Ten opponents afterward and fell completely to pieces. Notre Dame, however, was fortunate in having a weak Pitt team as its next adversary.

Later in the season the Irish barely beat a powerful Northwestern eleven, but when they went to Los Angeles for their final game, a perfect season seemed assured. Southern California had lost three times and did not appear to be a serious obstacle.

But the Trojans, as they had done in 1931, and as they would do again in 1964 and 1970, were about to put forth a superhuman effort against the overconfident Midwesterners. It was 14–7 with only four minutes left to play, and Southern Cal's white-shirted rooting section was going wild in anticipation of the season's greatest upset. But the Irish were not yet finished. A reserve halfback named Billy Gay took the Trojan kickoff and twisted his way down the field for 86 yards before being halted near the goal. Notre Dame scored and converted a moment later, and its undefeated record remained intact. The 14–14 tie, however, was a tremendous moral victory for the Trojans.

A year later the Irish had to resort to similar last-minute derring-do to save their fourth consecutive unbeaten season from ruin at the hands of an inspired Southern Methodist eleven. This time a tie was broken and Notre Dame won by a touchdown to complete a perfect ten-game campaign. A new quarterback, Bob Williams, had come along to direct the squad, which had retained most of its key linemen and backs. Williams was especially good at passing and ball handling, but the real star of the backfield was "Six-yard" Sitko, who easily lived up to his nickname while becoming the best running back in the nation.

Offensively, the 1949 team was the best that Leahy ever coached. Between the accurate passes of Williams and the quick opening thrusts of Sitko and the other backs, it was nearly impossible for a defense to stop the Irish.

In common with all of Leahy's creations, there was more emphasis on power than on finesse. There was, to be sure, the expert faking and timing which had come to be associated with the Leahy brand of T-formation maneuvers, but the real reason for Notre Dame's four-year undefeated span was its overwhelming superiority in blocking and tackling. Leahy himself had been an extremely aggressive lineman, and he constructed his championship teams in that image. He employed the Notre Dame football tradition expertly to motivate his players, while at the same time instilling enough poise so that they did not make many mistakes under stress.

As the Irish scaled new heights of accomplishment, every opponent reached its own emotional peak when playing them. There were no small-time teams on their schedule. Moreover, the immediate postwar years saw the caliber of athlete on nearly every campus reach its highest level. The players were older, steadier, more experienced, and did not vary in their week-to-week performance the way eighteen- and nineteen-year-olds did. Against such top-drawer competition, Notre Dame swept through thirty-nine games and four seasons without defeat in what must certainly stand as the greatest accomplishment in the modern history of the game.

Yet Leahy, riding atop this enormously successful machine, experienced a profound personal disappointment. He made the bitter and painful discovery that in a competitive system there is no law which says that the losers must like the winners. On occasion, of course, they might—especially when a man with the extraordinary attributes of a Rockne, or a Zuppke, or a Stagg, is at the top. But Leahy seemed to annoy some by his reticence and others by what they thought was his hypocritical arrogance. When he bemoaned the fate of the Irish on an approaching Saturday, his detractors, who knew that Notre Dame was a top-heavy favorite, railed at such false expressions of dread. Yet Leahy was merely invoking the age-old crying towel, which had been a part of coaching since Walter Camp's time. Then, too, there was his continual use of the term "lads" in describing the hulking giants who manned the Irish elevens. Somehow "lads" seemed inapplicable to the likes of a Ziggy Czarobski, or the tough marine veteran Jim Martin, or the 265-pound Leon Hart. Rockne could have used such a word and harvested a bumper crop of good cheer from the Fourth Estate, but all that Leahy got was a bad press. He was accused of being verbose and of trying to put on airs.

The hostility of so many writers and colleagues both mystified and wounded Leahy. Like most perfectionists, he was an intricate blend of anxiety, tension, and diffidence. If he employed a word such as "lads," it was because the term was common to the Dakotas of his boyhood, and he could not understand the testiness it provoked. And if he used the language well, albeit a bit overabundantly, it should not have triggered such enmity.

Whatever the underlying cause, the fact remains that Leahy never achieved the hold upon the public mind that Rockne attained. Probably no coach could have, but the reason that it was expected of Leahy more than of any other was that he was as much of a winner—and at the same university. Yet the times in which they coached were as different as any two eras could have been, and their personalities were, too. Frank Leahy made a record equal to Knute Rockne's, but not an impact.

A great coach always shows more of his genius when his team is suffering misfortune than he does when it is winning a national championship. This was true of Leahy after the fabulous undefeated streak ended with a dull thud in 1950. The Irish lost four games and were not blessed with

202

Notre Dame's Frank Leahy in one of his more relaxed moments.

their usual personnel. But all of the defeats were by close scores and, at least in the Michigan State game, the team put on a spectacular offensive show before going down 36–33.

It was in his last three seasons as coach that Leahy worked a near miracle at South Bend. The material was now only average, for the most part. And some of the schools on the schedule, notably Michigan State, Oklahoma, and Southern California, were better manned.

The Irish rebounded strongly in 1951, although losing by an awesome 35–0 margin to the unbeaten Michigan State Spartans in the worst defeat of Leahy's career. Seven games were won, however, with the only other defeat coming at the hands of Southern Methodist.

The next year Notre Dame accomplished the remarkable feat of beating four conference champions. Texas, Purdue, Oklahoma, and Southern California, each triumphant in its respective league, fell before the Irish. All of the games were close, with the decision in the Oklahoma battle hanging on a crushing tackle by Dan Shannon, which gave the Irish the ball in the last quarter and set the stage for a 27–21 victory. The superb running of the Sooners' Heisman Trophy winner, Billy Vessels, almost carried the day for Bud Wilkinson's high-scoring club. Twice the elusive Vessels broke away for long touchdown runs, but Notre Dame regained its composure each time and hung on to achieve a cherished victory.

The same tenacity on defense was the key to success in the Texas and Purdue games. Against Southern California, which was bidding for a perfect season in its last game, Notre Dame received an assist from cold weather and from the fact that the Trojans were somewhat flat after their big victory over U.C.L.A. on the preceding Saturday. Yet Southern Cal was certainly the stronger team on paper, and most observers thought that it would beat the Irish. Playing on the frozen turf at South Bend, the Notre Dame defense stopped U.S.C.'s off-tackle single-wing cutback and won a bitterly contested 9–0 victory.

To have defeated four conference champions in a single season was an achievement in itself worthy of a national title, but the Irish could not cope with Biggie Munn's great

Johnny Lattner of Notre Dame. Here the nation's best defensive back in 1953 carries the ball just to show how versatile he is.

Michigan State team and were defeated. They also fell upset victim to Pitt. Despite these losses, it was widely believed that Leahy's coaching and his team's playing during 1952 were the most inspired since the days of Rockne's last champions in 1930.

The secret of the brilliant accomplishment was defense, and the key to the defense was Johnny Lattner, a flawless performer who bore a considerable similarity to Lujack. Lattner ran well on offense, caught passes, and kicked effectively. But on defense he stood out as far and away the best back in the nation. He won the Heisman Trophy in 1953, even as Lujack had six years before, and with much the same knack of making the big interception or tackle when it was most needed.

With Lattner leading the team, Notre Dame stormed over opponents one after another in 1953 until it came to the Iowa game. The pressures of another undefeated record had been imposing a crushing strain upon Leahy. He had collapsed during halftime of the Georgia Tech game, and doctors were pleading with him to give up coaching.

Against Iowa it looked as though the unbeaten string was about to be broken. The Hawkeyes led by a touchdown with time running out in the first half. A Notre Dame player feigned injury, thus enabling the Irish to gain a few seconds. They used them well, tying the score. In the waning moments of the fourth quarter, after Iowa had regained the lead, the identical situation arose again, and the Irish managed to salvage a tie with the furious Hawkeyes.

But the tactics employed in deliberately faking injuries caused a widespread outburst of resentment. Notre Dame was criticized for poor sportsmanship. Its defenders insisted that what the Irish had done was nothing new, and they were correct. Teams, both before and since, have resorted to the same device to stop the clock. If people were more angry at Notre Dame than they might have been at another school, it stemmed either from the extreme of pure hatred or from an expectation that the premier institution in football would exhibit an ethical grandeur that matched its win-

206

ning percentage. And if it was sometimes terribly difficult to do both, that was the heart of Notre Dame's dilemma.

The season ended two weeks later, and Leahy celebrated another undefeated record by retiring. In eleven years under the Golden Dome, he had seen 87 victories and only 11 losses. Six of his teams had gone through unbeaten, two of them achieving perfect seasons, and no less than five times had the Irish claimed the national championship. Frank Leahy now stood second only to the immortal Rockne as a coaching success. But the bitch goddess, as always, had exacted her price.

24. Fritz Crisler's Masterpiece

Fritz Crisler wanted one more undefeated team before he called it a career. After seventeen years of coaching he had accomplished everything he had set out to do, with two exceptions: he had never taken a team to the Rose Bowl and he had never won a national championship.

Now, in 1947, he had high hopes of satisfying both ambitions. Crisler had begun to build his last great team three years before it ever took the field. The seventeen- and eighteen-year-old freshmen who played during the war years had gained invaluable experience. They were joined in 1946 by a host of discharged servicemen and the next year by a handful of especially good sophomores. The end result was one of the epic collections of football talent, not only in Michigan's history but in the annals of the game as well. The team represented the full flowering of Crisler's platoon concept. His offensive unit was speedy and maneuverable, with no one weighing more than 195 pounds. On defense Crisler sent in much bigger and stronger men, who nonetheless possessed considerable agility. The pursuit, always a hallmark of a good defense, was excellent.

But it was the offensive backfield which was Crisler's real pride and joy and the key to the team's point-scoring proficiency. At quarterback was the small (178 pounds), brilliant Howard Yerges, whose mind resembled a computer. He seemed to know each man's assignment on every one of Crisler's plays and exactly the right moment to confound a defense. Yerges may have inherited his signal-calling genius from his father, who quarterbacked the first Ohio State team that ever beat Michigan, back in the days of Chic Harley, in 1919.

The all-important tailback position was filled by Bob Chappuis, an Army Air Corps veteran who had been shot down in Italy during the war. For three months before being rescued, Chappuis had been hidden in an attic by local resistance leaders while, in the courtyard below, German soldiers streamed in and out of their company headquarters. Chappuis had been on the varsity in 1942 and was familiar with Crisler's offense. He was a stunningly accurate passer and, as the heaviest member of the backfield at 184 pounds, ran with strength and ingenuity.

At the opposite halfback was Chalmers "Bump" Elliott (later Michigan's coach), whose brother Pete (later Illinois' coach) was the second-string quarterback. The Elliotts' father had been an assistant coach at Northwestern. Bump, who weighed only 168 pounds, had played during the war at Purdue and was the perfect wingback in the Crisler scheme. He was especially good at catching passes, ran the essential reverse play with lightning quickness, and was probably the most versatile player on the entire squad.

The fullback position, possibly the most important of all, was manned by Jack Weisenberger, who had also played at tailback during the war. In Michigan's version of the single wing, the ball was usually centered directly to Weisenberger, who then set in motion the bewildering spinner cycle. He whirled and either handed the ball to the tailback or wingback, or kept it himself and started into the line. Here he could either plunge on through or slip the ball to the quarterback.

Weisenberger, a frail 178 pounds, was also capable of running around either end, since he had good speed. At deception he was without peer, masking his actions so cleverly that even the coaches could not be certain which of his colleagues had received the ball. This talent was the distinguishing feature of the backfield as a whole. It was the combination of versatility, speed, coordination, and ballhandling skill which made this quartet the most exciting backfield since the Four Horsemen. They and their teammates were indeed the "Magicians" that the sportswriters had nicknamed them. There had been other deceptive offenses in football before, but the 1947 Wolverines reached a pinnacle in the art of sleight of hand that has never been equaled.

Crisler's men operated from seven different formations and turned loose a stupefying array of full spinners, half spinners, buck laterals, reverses, end arounds, and quick openers, on many of which three and sometimes even four men handled the ball. The players reveled in such complexity and knew that theirs was something special in the long tradition of hidden-ball offenses that stretched back to the days of Percy Haughton.

Michigan swept through its season, piling up almost unbelievable scores. A good Michigan State team was obliterated 55–0. Pittsburgh was handed the worst defeat in its history, 69–0. Stanford and Northwestern were buried under seven-touchdown avalanches. Only Minnesota—playing an inspired game, with its huge line led by Leo Nomellini and Clayton Tonnemaker—and a tough Illinois team succeeded in holding down the score. Michigan defeated each by a touchdown, then went on to devastate Indiana, Wisconsin, and Ohio State. The Wolverines scored 345 points, the most a Big Ten team had run up since the turn of the century, and allowed nine opponents only 53. All that remained now was for this collection of "chrome-plated, hand-tooled specialists," as *Time Magazine* had called them, to make their appearance in the Rose Bowl.

The Big Ten and the Pacific Coast Conference had entered into an agreement to send their respective champions to Pasadena, with the provision that no team could go twice in succession. Illinois and U.C.L.A. had started the series the year before. The Bruins, with a perfect record, wanted to play Army's glamour team, and Coast fans and writers deprecated the Illini. This was all coach Ray Eliot needed to motivate his twice-beaten club. With Perry Moss passing and the unstoppable Claude "Buddy" Young galloping at will through the Bruins, the angry Midwesterners roared to a 45–14 victory.

Coach Herbert Orin "Fritz" Crisler
instructs the gentlemen of Princeton
in the proper procedure for
knocking someone down.

Illinois had been a badly underrated team, but no one in the West made the same mistake about Michigan. The Coast champion, Southern California, had lost only to Notre Dame, but by a 38–7 score. Michigan realized that its showing against the Trojans was its only chance to make the sportswriters reconsider their award of the national championship to Notre Dame. Crisler had his platoons at their emotional and physical peak for the school's first appearance in Pasadena since Yost's point-a-minute men had played in the inaugural forty-six years before.

It is doubtful, however, if even the most confident Michigan follower could have imagined the heights his team would reach. The Wolverines won by exactly the same margin as Yost's team had: 49–0. They scored seven touchdowns, three by Weisenberger, and "Automatic" Jim Brieske kicked 7 extra points with the same calm skill he had shown all season. The offensive maneuvers completely baffled the Trojans, who ran in circles trying to find out who had the ball. When they did, it was always too late. And on those rare occasions when Southern California had possession, usually after a Michigan touchdown, its backs were brought to earth by Len Ford, Alvin Wistert, and the crushing linebackers Dan Dworsky and Dick Kempthorn. And when the Trojans punted, Gene Derricotte, the best return artist in the nation, rambled for huge gains.

Chappuis found that it was easy to pass to his sure-handed ends, Bob Mann and Dick Rifenburg. And Michigan's watch-charm guards, Dominic Tomasi and Stuart Wilkins, demonstrated the requisite speed in pulling out of the line to lead the running plays. Crisler had always maintained that good running guards were crucial to the success of his precision offense, and now he was watching the two best he had ever seen.

All things considered, the superiority in every phase of the game exhibited by the Wolverines marked them as one of the great teams of all time. Never had one sectional champion so totally defeated another. Crisler, who was seldom given to overstatement, said that it had been the best performance by the finest team he had ever coached. And the

Claude "Buddy" Young of Illinois carries the ball for a big gain against Wisconsin in the 1946 game at Champaign. The Illini won 27–21 and went to the Rose Bowl.

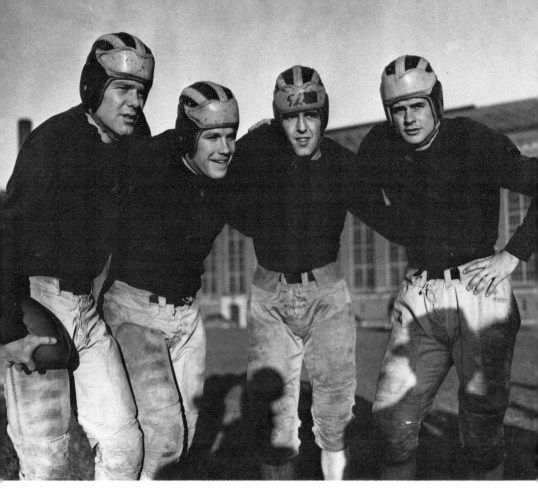

The Magicians, Michigan's 1947 backfield. From left, Chalmers "Bump" Elliott, Howard Yerges, Jack Weisenberger, and Bob Chappuis.

master architect of the language, Red Smith, wrote that it would be a sacrilege to mention any other college team in the same breath with Michigan.

It was no surprise, then, that the Wolverine faithful put enormous pressure on the Associated Press to take another poll. It did, although it was considered unofficial, and this time Michigan was named national champion by an overwhelming majority of the sportswriters.

Now it was the Notre Dame partisans who were miffed. They accused Crisler of running up a score. Michigan men answered that both the Wolverines and the Irish had made

28 points in the second half. The arguments were endless and settled nothing. Southern Cal had played better against Notre Dame, trailing by only a field goal at the half, whereas in the Rose Bowl it was behind by 21–0.

Grantland Rice thought that Notre Dame had a stronger line but that Michigan had better backs, greater deception, a superior passing game, and more reserve strength. What was beyond doubt, however, was that 1947 saw two of the finest elevens ever to play the game.

There was now only one more item on Crisler's agenda: resignation. He thus ended his decade at Ann Arbor with a record of 71 victories and 16 defeats. Moreover, he had changed Michigan's concept of winning football. Gone was the idea of playing for the other team's mistakes. Crisler had made the offense paramount in Michigan's thinking.

He stepped up to become athletic director, and Bennie Oosterbaan became Michigan's head coach. Oosterbaan had been in charge of the backfield and before that had coached the ends, at which position he himself had been the university's most celebrated athlete in the mid-twenties.

The new coach inherited an almost intact defense, but graduation had decimated the high-scoring offensive unit. Oosterbaan quickly elevated Pete Elliott to the starting quarterback position and Tom Peterson to fullback. Then he installed a pair of sophomores, Chuck Ortmann and Leo Koceski, at the vital tailback and wingback posts. Ortmann was a perfect choice as a successor to Chappuis. He could pass with great accuracy and run the off-tackle play with considerable power. Koceski turned out to be a sparkling pass receiver and a swift runner on the key reverse play.

The Wolverines rolled through their nine-game schedule without defeat or tie to register a second perfect season and win the national championship. They were not as dazzling a team on offense as their celebrated predecessors had been, but they still managed to score 252 points. On defense, however, they were even better, allowing only 44.

Having played for Yost, Oosterbaan had a deep appreciation of defensive football. In the game that meant the Big Ten championship, Northwestern's strong team was shut out 28–0. Ortmann enjoyed a field day in passing to Koceski for three touchdowns. The Wolverines also managed to contain the aerial attack of Norman VanBrocklin while stopping Oregon's Pacific Coast co-champions 14–0.

The team had close games with Michigan State, Illinois, and Ohio State, but came up with the big play when it was needed. Ortmann threw a 51-yard touchdown pass to another sophomore, Harry Allis, to keep the Illini from ruining the season. The same combination produced a 44-yard scoring pass to highlight the victory over Ohio State. Oosterbaan thus became one of the few coaches ever to achieve a perfect season in his first year.

Most of the stars had graduated by 1949, but the Wolverines continued to win in the conference. They saw their victory streak snapped at twenty-five, however, by Army. Throughout the season Michigan found it difficult to score, and only a determined defense enabled it to upset a vastly superior Minnesota eleven and preserve a tie for the Big Ten title with Ohio State.

By 1950 the remarkable championship cycle had run its course, and no one expected the Wolverines to win a fourth Big Ten crown in succession. But they did, earning it in a fantastic blizzard at Columbus, where they defeated Ohio State without making a first down.

The weather conditions were so bad that the game was nearly canceled. It turned into a contest of blocked kicks, with a 24-inch snowfall, 10-degree temperatures, and a 30-mile-an-hour gale combining to make any maneuvering impossible. Despite the weather, more than 50,000 Buckeye fans sat in the stadium. Many of them criticized coach Wes Fesler bitterly for allowing his team to punt from deep in its territory with only seconds remaining in the half. Michigan, trailing 3–2 at the time, blocked the kick on a splendid effort by Tony Momsen, who then recovered it behind Ohio State's goal line for a touchdown. Ortmann punted consistently throughout the second half to preserve the lead and ensure Michigan of the Big Ten championship and a bid to the Rose Bowl.

Despite having lost three games and tied one, the Wolverines were not as weak a team as the West Coast observers thought. Injuries had reduced their effectiveness all year, and with a month in which to recuperate they were confident of facing unbeaten California in their best physical condition of the season.

The Golden Bears dominated the first half, but Ortmann came back in the final quarter to pitch screen passes to his fullback Don Dufek and long strikes to end Lowell Perry. Trailing 6–0 late in the game, Michigan finally scored, and when Allis kicked the extra point, the outcome was decided. California's fourth-down desperation pass deep in its territory failed and Michigan was handed a gift touchdown that made the final score 14–6. Ortmann had completed fifteen of nineteen passes, and the Wolverine defense had contained California's powerful running game in the second half.

For the easygoing and friendly Oosterbaan, who enjoyed extraordinary rapport with his players, it marked the end of a three-season cycle in which he had coached the varsity to one perfect season and national title, three conference championships, and a Rose Bowl triumph. Although he would turn out several strong teams in his remaining eight years as coach at Ann Arbor, including those led by the great Ron Kramer, the best end of the decade, this was the high point for Oosterbaan.

25. Red Blaik's Finest Hour

The coming of peace to the plains of West Point did not signal the decline of Army's football fortunes as so many had predicted it would. Red Blaik showed that he still had the championship touch by turning out an undefeated team in 1948 and an unbeaten, untied eleven the following year.

But there were a few disappointments in that first season after Blanchard and Davis had graduated. There was a totally unexpected loss to Columbia, 21–20, in a wild finish that saw the Lions' great pass catcher Bill Swiacki make one seemingly impossible reception after another. The defeat ended Army's unbeaten streak at thirty-two games. Then there was the bad afternoon at South Bend when Notre Dame thrashed the Cadets to gain some measure of revenge for its wartime humiliations.

But when Blaik installed the deft Arnold Galiffa as his T-formation quarterback, the Black Knights began to roll once again. They were not the monsters of the war years, but they were nonetheless a sound football team, well-drilled and meticulously organized in the traditional Red Blaik manner.

There was some criticism of their schedules for being padded with decidedly second-rate opposition, but the Cadets argued in rebuttal that the commitments had been made years in advance and that they could not be blamed for the decline of material at schools such as Harvard and Fordham. Still it was true that there were games with the likes of Villanova, New Mexico, Washington and Lee, and

218

Davidson, which were not—and had never been—gridiron giants.

Army stopped a strong Illinois team in a big game early in the 1948 campaign, then went on to hand Cornell its only defeat of the year. Pennsylvania was beaten on a last-second touchdown. The only remaining obstacle to a perfect season was a Navy team which had lost all eight of its games.

The Cadets were top-heavy favorites and there was nothing that Blaik could do to get them to take the Navy seriously. An attack of food poisoning swept through the Army players on the eve of the game, but they were not prevented from appearing. The Midshipmen, totally unaware that they did not belong on the same field with the mighty Cadets, scored three touchdowns and had a like number scored on them. The game ended in a 21–21 tie, which was considered the moral victory of the year for Navy and the shock of the year for the odds makers.

The next season, with Galiffa in full stride as the nation's best quarterback and Dan Foldberg and Elmer Stout starring in the line, the Cadets justified all their advance billing by winning every game. They got too much credit for beating a Michigan team that was only a remnant of its great predecessors, but they were not praised highly enough for their awesome 38–0 rout of Navy, the greatest victory in the long history of the rivalry.

In 1950 the Army was just as good, rolling up huge scores against its weaker adversaries and winning by smaller but convincing margins over Michigan, Pennsylvania, and Stanford. Galiffa had graduated, but Blaik's son Bob proved to be a more than adequate replacement. The Cadets had a powerful running game with Al Pollard leading the charge, and with Bob Blaik's artful passing, their offense was perfectly balanced.

By the time they went to Philadelphia for the Navy game, they were on the verge of a second consecutive perfect season and a third without defeat. In three years only the tie with Navy marred the record. Army was again a staggering favorite over the Midshipmen. All the Navy had was a hard-running quarterback named Bob Zastrow and a great deal of suppressed hostility over its humiliation of the year before. But it was enough. Navy won 14–2 in one of the great upsets of all time. For the crestfallen Cadets there was not even the consolation of a little food poisoning. Years later Colonel Blaik would take out the films of the debacle whenever he felt that his troops were growing overconfident, and for the Army it was always a horror movie.

But as great a calamity as the defeat was, it was as nothing compared to what befell West Point after the season ended. Some ninety cadets, including Blaik's son, were forced to resign for violations of academic discipline. Practically the entire football team was sent away, and a storm of controversy broke over the Academy. There were many who felt that the officials had been much too severe. The alleged inflexibility of the military mind was roundly condemned, and the justice of the West Point system itself was seriously questioned. Others insisted that the ousted Cadets had broken the rules and deserved expulsion. There seemed to be no middle ground in the dispute.

For Red Blaik it was a time of personal torment such as few coaches have ever known. No one would have condemned him if he had left to accept one of the numerous offers from other schools. But the grim Colonel walked the lonely battlements above the Hudson, stared down his grief, and stayed to give the Army football team pride in itself once again.

In the process, he exhibited perhaps the greatest coaching skill of his long career. Taking a virtual scrub team in 1951, he had the Cadets fighting for every game. They were overwhelmed by Navy, but the following year they did better, and in 1953 Blaik brought off a near miracle by turning out a club that lost only to Northwestern.

The Army fielded good teams in the mid-fifties, and despite two horrendous lickings at Michigan's hands, it was obvious that the Black Knights were again building up their forces for another assault on the national championship. Led by two great halfbacks, Bob Anderson and Pete Dawkins, the Heisman Trophy winner, the Cadets swept through the 1958 season, winning a cherished victory over Notre Dame at South Bend. Anderson and Dawkins, who looked like a latter-day Blanchard and Davis, ended the season in triumphant style with a 22–6 decision over the Navy. Only a tie with Pitt kept them from perfection.

But Blaik was satisfied. He had brought the Army all the way back. He retired after eighteen years, with a record of 121 victories and 33 defeats at West Point. He had earned a place, along with Leahy and Crisler, in the triumverate that dominated the profession in the forties.

26. Southerners Triumphant

The Southwest had waited a decade for another Heisman Trophy winner to come along and match the achievements of Davey O'Brien. In 1948 its patience was rewarded in the person of Doak Walker, who did everything for S.M.U. that "Slingshot" Davey had done for Texas Christian.

Walker carried the Mustangs to an undefeated season in 1947 and to the Cotton Bowl both that year and the next. He caught passes, ran back punts and kickoffs, bounded past defenders in his deceptive style, and played defense with rare skill. He did not match O'Brien when it came to throwing the ball, but then neither had anyone else in the Southwest, except Sammy Baugh.

Walker possessed that indefinable attribute which all great athletes have that enables them to make the big play at the crucial moment in a game. He did it against arch rival Texas in 1947 as the Mustangs beat a strong team quarterbacked by Walker's old high school colleague Bobby Layne.

Two years in succession against fired-up T.C.U., Walker combined with the accurate passer Gil Johnson to pull Southern Methodist back from the brink of defeat and salvage ties. Against Oregon in the 1949 Cotton Bowl, he put on a typical show, punting flawlessly, dancing through the Webfoots as though he had eyes in the back of his head, and kicking a pair of extra points.

Those who saw Walker run in the open field marveled at his dodging ability, which confounded tacklers who knew as well as everyone else did that he lacked great speed. De-

Bobby Layne of Texas in 1947. If only he could have avoided his old pal Doak Walker and S.M.U., it would have been a perfect season.

fenders often had several chances to stop Walker, but it did not seem to bother him. He got away no matter how often they lunged.

Walker had great help in putting the Mustangs into the 1949 Cotton Bowl from a sensational sophomore named Kyle Rote. When the two were healthy, S.M.U. was the most dangerous offensive team in the country. But in his last year Walker was injured much of the time, and as the final game with Notre Dame's invincible national champions drew near, it looked as though a carnage was about to take place. Rote, however, stepped into the spotlight, and with a wildly aroused supporting cast, almost brought off the upset of the century. The Irish had to rally in the closing moments to win 27–20 in the most thrilling game of the season. In defeat the Mustangs, especially the valiant Rote, were the toast of the Southwest and much of the rest of the nation as well. Even in shaken South Bend they were accorded considerable respect.

Rote could do just about everything Walker could and was perhaps even better at catching passes. When Fred Benners came along to throw the ball with such stunning accuracy, Rote and the other Mustang receivers came into their own. It was Benners who engineered the big upset victory over Ohio State in the 1950 opener.

In the years since, Southern Methodist has emphasized the aerial game perhaps more than any other team. It has unbalanced the school's offense so that opponents usually can forget about any running threat and concentrate on pass defense. But if it has cost the Mustangs some games, it has made them one of the most exciting elevens in the country to watch.

The passing game was emphasized also by Georgia under coach Wallace Butts. With Johnny Rauch and Charlie Trippi leading the club in 1946, Georgia won every game and defeated North Carolina in the Sugar Bowl.

The Tarheels were a strong eleven dominated by a player who closely resembled Doak Walker in his versatility. He was Charlie "Choo-Choo" Justice, the greatest performer ever developed at Chapel Hill. As a single wing tailback, Justice

That's S.M.U.'s Doak Walker with the ball, and a number of determined Pitt Panthers trying to head him off at the pass.

excelled as a runner, passer, and kicker. Like Walker, he was not fast, but compensated with an adroit change of pace in the open field. He also was a durable defensive back who often played the entire game, even in an era of free substitution. Throughout the late forties opponents concentrated their defenses on the Tarheel star, but North Carolina won anyway, as Justice could seldom be denied.

For years the powerful Southeast Conference had produced hordes of flashy offensive players, but in the fifties it began to turn its attention to defense with gratifying results.

At Georgia Tech, coach Robert Lee Dodd, who had been a great quarterback at Tennessee under General Neyland in the late twenties, turned out unusually strong elevens. With Darrell Crawford and Leon Hardiman in the backfield, the Engineers went unbeaten in 1951, although tied by Duke. The following season they compiled the finest record in the history of the school by winning eleven regular-season games and defeating Mississippi in the Sugar Bowl.

Dodd was a remarkable coach in that he believed that football should be an enjoyable activity for his players. Thus his philosophy differed from that of men such as Bierman, Sutherland, Dobie, and his own coach, Neyland, who saw the game more as something resembling a war of attrition than as a pleasurable pastime. Dodd created a relaxed atmosphere among his athletes, whom he treated with enormous consideration. The morale of his teams was always high, and they performed unusually well under stress.

Dodd emphasized deception on offense, and with consistently good passing from Crawford the Engineers were well-balanced on the attack. But it was the stubborn defense which was the key to the success of the two undefeated teams. Tech did not have the biggest linemen in the conference by any means but it did have the quickest. Dodd always looked first for a defensive man's ability to react to sudden movements by the opponents. He knew that pursuit and good tackling were at the heart of a sound defense. In this respect he was only following the dicta of General Neyland.

Within a few years other conference coaches, such as Paul "Bear" Bryant at Alabama, Ralph "Shug" Jordan at

Charlie "Choo Choo" Justice of North Carolina. For the Tarheels, this was the little engine that could.

Kyle Rote of S.M.U. runs against Notre Dame's national champions in the almost-upset at Dallas in 1949.

Auburn, Bowden Wyatt at Tennessee, Paul Dietzel at Louisiana State, and John Vaught at Mississippi, were fielding the finest overall collection of defensive teams in the nation.

Dietzel, in particular, received considerable publicity for his "Chinese Bandits" at Baton Rouge. They were a special unit which concentrated solely on stopping the other side, and they made an essential contribution to the Bengal Tigers' national championship record in 1958. Dietzel also had strong ballcarriers, such as Billy Cannon and Jim Taylor, but once again it was defense that made the difference in the crucial games. Seven points were enough to turn back a spirited Clemson team in the Sugar Bowl.

A touchdown was also sufficient for the Tennessee Volunteers of coach Bowden Wyatt to win their classic struggle with Georgia Tech in 1956. It was the season's most important game, with perfect records on the line. Johnny Majors, a triple-threat tailback, was Tennessee's star player all year. But for Wyatt, who had learned nearly all there was to know about defense while leading another undefeated team at Knoxville eighteen years before, the only real way to cope with the Engineers was to out-pursue and out-tackle them for sixty full minutes. This is exactly what his team did in a much-celebrated 6–0 victory.

An unyielding defense brought Auburn its national championship in 1957 as the Plainsmen beat Tennessee 7–0, Kentucky 6–0, Georgia Tech 3–0, and Georgia 6–0. They allowed ten opponents a total of only 28 points. In a time of such sophisticated offenses and with so many good forward passers in the game, the defensive record of coach Jordan's eleven was astonishing.

Alabama soon discovered that the best way to supplant Auburn was to build an even better defense. Bear Bryant was brought back to his alma mater from Texas A. & M., where he had taught the Aggies how to shut out opponents with a regularity they had not equaled since before the war. Now Bryant did the same for the Crimson Tide. His 1961 national champions were even better than Auburn, permitting only 22 points in ten games. Three touchdowns and a field goal were all that the opposition could score against a de-

Joe Namath of Alabama in 1962. The knees were healthy then, and the defense always had to worry about an end run.

fensive unit led by the best linebacker in the country, Lee Roy Jordan. Alabama featured a good passing game during these years, with Joe Namath being the best of the quarterbacks.

Bryant's quick-reacting teams continued to dominate the Southeast during the sixties, as the Tide claimed two more national titles and twice defeated strong Nebraska clubs in the Sugar Bowl. Only at the end of the decade, when he began to run short of the speedy recruits he liked so much, did Bryant's elevens begin to falter.

Always keen rivals for sectional honors were the Mississippi machines turned out by John Vaught, the onetime All-America guard from Texas Christian. Backfield stars, such as Charlie Flowers, Jake Gibbs, and Glynn Griffing, gave the Rebels a high-scoring offense. But Vaught's forte, along with the other leading coaches in the conference, was defense. The 1959 team allowed only 21 points in ten games, yet it was beaten by arch rival L.S.U. Mississippi held a 3–0 lead late in the fourth quarter on Halloween night when the Bengal Tigers' Billy Cannon took a punt back 89 yards for the winning touchdown. Nearly every man on the Rebel squad had a chance to stop Cannon, but none could as the Heisman Trophy winner made one of the epic dashes in football history.

Mississippi, however, was so convinced that it was really the better team that it arranged to play L.S.U. again, in the Sugar Bowl. The Rebels were proven correct on New Year's Day when they avenged their earlier defeat by a one-sided 21–0 margin.

27. A New Kind of T

For the first few years after the modern T formation revolutionized offensive football, most coaches were content merely to understand it and not to try any modifications. At the University of Missouri, however, the inventive Don Faurot began tinkering with the new system and came up with something even more explosive.

Faurot did two things: he increased the space between the linemen and he employed the quarterback as a runner. The wider spacing—or splits—gave the linemen better blocking angles and forced the defense to cover a broader front.

But it was the new use of the quarterback that made the "split T" formation so exciting. Where before he would merely turn around and either hand the ball or fake to a halfback, now the quarterback ran along the line of scrimmage parallel to the defense. If the opposing end rushed in, the quarterback turned and pitched the ball to a trailing halfback. If the defensive end refrained from charging, the quarterback could keep the ball himself and cut to the inside while the halfback blocked the end out of the play. There was also a passing option by either back, and there were virtually unlimited opportunities for variations.

Faurot had been using the single wing at Missouri, where he had the nation's best passer, Paul Christman, in 1939. During the war years Faurot had a chance to perfect his ideas while coaching naval preflight teams. His two key assistants, Bud Wilkinson and Jim Tatum, were fascinated by the new formation and later made it the basis of their own offenses when they became head coaches at Oklahoma and Maryland respectively.

Much of the success that Wilkinson enjoyed during a seventeen-year tenure at Oklahoma, in which his teams won 145 games and lost only 29, can be traced to the devastating use of the split T formation. He seemed to have an abundance of precisely the right players to make it work most effectively. The linemen were rangy and quick, racing downfield to deliver the blocks that set the fast-moving halfbacks free for long scoring dashes. And at the vital quarterback position Wilkinson had a parade of excellent players. Jack Mitchell, Darrell Royal, and Claude Arnold all possessed the attributes he sought in a split-T signal caller.

The formation was principally designed for rushing, and Wilkinson had swift halfbacks, such as Billy Vessels, Tommy McDonald, and Clendon Thomas, to outrun the befuddled defenders. In Leon Heath and Buck McPhail the Sooners had fullbacks who combined strong blocking with great speed on the quick opening plays. But all of these star backs would have gone nowhere without the superior Oklahoma lines coached by Gomer Jones, the old Ohio State All-America center. Jones was in the tradition of Wilkinson's own line coach in his playing days at Minnesota, Dr. George Hauser.

The Sooner forwards dominated the All-America lists with such nominees as Jim Owens and Max Boydston at end, Wade Walker and Jim Weatherall at tackle, Paul Burris and J. D. Roberts at guard, and Jerry Tubbs at center.

With this wealth of talent and Wilkinson's genius for organization, motivation, and preparation, it was no surprise when Oklahoma thundered through the Big Seven. In Wilkinson's first thirteen years as coach, the Sooners won the conference title every time, compiling 70 victories and 2 ties without a loss.

Nonconference opposition, however, was much more difficult, and, in fact, Oklahoma beat Notre Dame only once in six games under Wilkinson. Both excursions into the Big Ten, against strong Northwestern teams, also ended in defeat.

There were some who denigrated the Sooners' great victory streaks by pointing out that the caliber of Big Seven play was far below that of the other conferences. But Oklahoma did well in bowl games, where it defeated North Carolina, Louisiana State, Duke, and Maryland. The games with Jim Tatum's Terrapins in the Orange Bowl in 1954 and 1956, which Oklahoma won 7–0 and 20–6 respectively, had national championship implications.

Wilkinson had, altogether, four perfect-record teams and six others which lost but a single game. Three of these squads were denied unbeaten seasons by Notre Dame, one by Santa Clara, one by Texas, and one by Kentucky.

The longest winning streak in football history, 47 games, was achieved by the teams from 1954 through 1957. Notre Dame went to Norman and finally ended it by a 7–0 score. Another victory string extended to 31 games from 1948 to the Sugar Bowl game of 1951.

The Sooners met defeat at New Orleans when the astute Bear Bryant devised a defense that checked the split T, enabling Kentucky to stage a 13–7 upset. Bryant gave his standout defensive end Walter Yowarsky the job of tracking Oklahoma's quarterback, Claude Arnold, wherever he went. The strategy was splendidly conceived and perfectly executed by Yowarsky, who buffeted Arnold all afternoon. The timing of the Sooners' running plays was upset and fumbles resulted. Yowarsky received vital support from Kentucky's great tackle Bob Gain, and Oklahoma found it virtually impossible to generate the kind of sustained marches that had carried it to a national championship.

Bryant had demonstrated one method of coping with the split T, but it required the talents of a Yowarsky and a Gain, and few squads were so well supplied. Occasionally a team with speedy linebackers found that it could send them through the wide spaces in the split T offensive line and into the backfield in time to disrupt the plays before they started. But this was risky business, since it left vast open spaces in the secondary, thus enabling a runner who broke through the line quickly to go for a touchdown.

Nothing like this happened to Kentucky, however, and Bryant earned one of his most cherished victories. He had

Charles "Bud" Wilkinson of Oklahoma, the premier coach of the 1950s.

become the master defensive strategist of the South, taking over from General Neyland, whose Tennessee teams he somehow could never manage to defeat.

Wilkinson's elevens rolled up huge scores during 1955 and 1956, years in which they were named national champions. The 1956 team ran up 466 points against ten opponents to become the highest-scoring club in Sooner history. It averaged nearly 400 yards' rushing in each game.

When the material finally declined and the secrets of success became common property, Oklahoma began losing games to the University of Texas, coached by Wilkinson's former quarterback Darrell Royal. The Sooners entered a lean cycle in which even their previously unchallenged hegemony in the Big Seven was overthrown. The caliber of the conference began to improve dramatically as Nebraska under Bob Devaney and Missouri under Dan Devine reasserted themselves.

In common with many of the other great coaches, Wilkinson revealed the amazing depth of his skill while working with less successful teams. Even in defeat, the Sooners retained the poise which was so much a personal characteristic of their coach.

Wilkinson also was unusual among his contemporaries for having wide interests in nonathletic areas. While at Syracuse as an assistant, he had earned a Master's degree in English. He was thus continuing an old Sooner tradition of scholarly football coaches. Back at the turn of the century, the team had been instructed by a young professor, fresh from Harvard, named Vernon Louis Parrington. He turned out three undefeated teams, then abandoned the game and the school to take up residence at the University of Washington. It was there that Parrington wrote his monumental *Main Currents in American Thought*, the classic work on the intellectual history of the United States.

28. Woody, Evy, and Biggie

The split T formation made a tremendous impression upon Big Ten coaches, especially upon those at Ohio State, Iowa, and Michigan State. These were the schools which also had the best material during the decade of the fifties.

At Columbus a new man had come to replace the Buckeyes' three-time All-America Wes Fesler, who had run into difficulty because his teams could not beat Michigan. His replacement was a big, flamboyant reader of von Clausewitz and Emerson's essays named Wayne Woodrow Hayes. A graduate of Denison University at Granville, Ohio, Woody Hayes had begun his coaching career in the picturesque community of Mingo Junction. He moved steadily upward from there and finally won the top job at the celebrated seedbed of successful coaches, Miami University in Oxford, Ohio.

Hayes inherited a good team at Ohio State in 1951, led by the Heisman Trophy winner, Vic Janowicz. But it was not to be the Buckeyes' year. Illinois, under Ray Eliot, came up with its best team in a generation and rolled through the Big Ten without defeat.

By the time that Hayes was in his fourth year, however, the Buckeyes were the best team in the country. His offense was keyed to a former Columbus high school star who reminded the old-timers of the immortal Chic Harley. What Howard "Hopalong" Cassady shared with the first Buckeye hero was the rare ability to turn a game around on one play. He did this on the two occasions in 1954 when it meant the difference between victory and defeat.

In the Wisconsin game the unbeaten Badgers and their crushing fullback, Heisman Trophy winner Alan Ameche, led 7–3 and were deep in Buckeye territory on the verge of the touchdown that would have given them an insurmountable advantage. Cassady, however, intercepted a pass on his 12-yard line and carried it all the way back for the score that destroyed Wisconsin's composure. Ohio State then went on to win by 17 points.

In the finale against Michigan, Cassady ran 60 yards after the Buckeyes had made a great stand at their goal line late in the fourth quarter. His dash set up the touchdown that broke a deadlock and gave Ohio State a perfect season.

Some fans and writers criticized Hayes for lack of imagination in his offense. "Three yards and a cloud of dust" was the scornful phrase they used, but those who had to face the Buckeye bulldozer accorded it grudging respect.

Hayes liked to batter opponents with his fullbacks moving behind devastating blocking. In Jim Parker he had one of the all-time great guards, and whenever a vital yard was needed, the backs followed him and always got it.

The running quarterback was another hallmark of the Ohio State offense. There was little need to pass, Hayes believed, as long as the ball could be moved on the ground. The strategy bored the spectators but it won football games.

Cassady led the team to another conference title in 1955 while picking up the Heisman Trophy. In the crucial game against Michigan, the Ohio State defense was impregnable and the Wolverines were shut out, deprived of a tie for the championship, and denied a Rose Bowl trip all in one afternoon. For the Columbus faithful—who regarded Ann Arbor with an ancient hostility born of monstrous indignities suffered at the hands of Yost and Crisler—it was a retribution to be savored.

It now began to look as though no one in the Big Ten could stop the Ohio State juggernaut. But at Iowa City the Hawkeyes were beginning to rise again with their best manpower since the days of Howard Jones in the early twenties.

Forest "Evy" Evashevski, the Iowa coach, had become fascinated with what his old Michigan teammate Dave Nel-

son was doing with the T formation. Nelson, coach at the University of Delaware, placed a halfback outside the end and thus opened up a whole new concept of reverse plays, pass patterns, and blocking angles. His innovation, which was based on an earlier theory of Lou Little's, seemed to combine the best features of both the T and the single wing formations. If football were philosophy, it might have been considered a Hegelian synthesis, but the sportswriters just called it the wing T.

Evashevski made additional refinements to suit the excellent personnel he had recruited. With adept passing quarterbacks such as Ken Ploen, Wilburn Hollis, and especially Randy Duncan, the Hawkeyes placed much more emphasis on the aerial game than did Ohio State in the years from 1956 to 1960. Duncan was the nation's best quarterback in 1958.

The Iowa lines, featuring Alex Karras, were both large and agile. Iowa's greatest lineman, Calvin Jones, was the foremost player in 1954 and 1955, seasons in which the Hawkeyes gave champion Ohio State strong opposition. Jones entered the Canadian football league after graduation and, in a strange and terrible caprice of fate which linked him with that other Hawkeye immortal, Nile Kinnick, was killed in an airliner crash.

During the five-season span from 1956 to 1960, Iowa won three Big Ten championships and two Rose Bowl games. The passing of the quarterbacks, complemented by an irresistible running game, made the Hawkeyes the most exciting offensive team in the country.

Iowa was also defensively outstanding in winning the championship in 1956, but a year later it was an inability to contain Ohio State's All-America fullback Bob White which cost the Hawkeyes the Big Ten title. With the score 13–10 in Iowa's favor late in the fourth quarter, White began slamming through the line. Seven times in eight plays he carried the ball as the Buckeyes marched 68 yards to the touchdown that won the conference championship. Iowa knew who would get the ball and where he was going, but noth-

Ohio State's Woody Hayes, of whom it has been said: "He is indomitable in defeat, insufferable in victory." The Scarlet and Gray carpet reminded his Buckeyes of their 1969 upset at Ann Arbor. They took the hint. In 1970 it was Ohio State 20, Michigan 9.

ing could stop the great Ohio State fullback. A year later he put on another one-man show to beat the Hawkeyes again, but this time Iowa had the title in its possession before the game.

The football being played at Iowa City was both fundamentally sound and exciting for the spectators. At East Lansing the Michigan State Spartans were also achieving success by combining the same elements. First under Clarence "Biggie" Munn and then under Hugh "Duffy" Daugherty, they produced two national champions with perfect records and four teams which lost only one game each. Included were a pair of hard-won Rose Bowl victories over exceptionally good U.C.L.A. teams.

The Spartans did not enter the Big Ten until the 1953 season, Munn's last as coach. He had been an All-America guard at Minnesota in the early thirties, then moved to Michigan as line coach for Fritz Crisler. When Michigan State decided to improve its football reputation, Munn, then at Syracuse, was given the task. It was slow going at first, as the dominant university at Ann Arbor seemed to be an invincible foe. But Munn's teams gradually narrowed the margin of their defeats, and in 1950 his Spartans finally overthrew Michigan 14–7.

From then on Michigan State became the strongest team in the area. The Spartans discovered that they could defeat Notre Dame as well, and continued to beat both the old titans of Midwestern football with monotonous regularity through the sixties.

In 1951 and 1952 Munn's three-deep squad beat everyone else too. These were the teams led by Al Dorow and Don McAuliffe in the backfield and Bob Carey and Don Coleman in the line. Coleman, at only 185 pounds, was a watch-charm tackle, but his explosive blocking ability made him by far the best offensive lineman in the country.

The Spartans used a variety of offensive formations, including the regular T, the split T, and the single wing. Munn called his system the multiple offense, and it meant multiple confusion for any defense that had to face it. Some critics said that when Michigan State met a Big Ten schedule it

Alan Ameche of Wisconsin. They called him the Horse, and whenever he got the ball, the Horse knew the way.

Hugh "Duffy" Daugherty of Michigan State. "Football," he once said, "is not a contact sport. Dancing is a contact sport. Football is a collision sport."

would learn humility, but in 1953 the winning streak grew still longer. It reached twenty-eight when Purdue finally ended it in a monumental 6–0 upset. The Purdue touchdown, ironically, was scored by Dan Pobojewski, who had transferred from Michigan State. The Boilermakers spoiled another Spartan bid for a perfect season in 1957 and became something of a jinx team for Michigan State.

Daugherty, who had played in the line at Syracuse when Munn was coaching there, took over in 1954. He had a succession of strong teams with such players as Earl Morrall, Walter Kowalczyk, and George Saimes in the backfield. Daugherty's elevens were much like Munn's, with the same spirit, poise, and wealth of offensive maneuvers. But each year it seemed that some underdog came along and ruined

Howard "Hopalong" Cassady. Touch-downs galore for the Buckeyes, and a memory for the old-timers of the one and only Chic Harley.

their season. Purdue, Minnesota, and Illinois all won games from the Spartans when they were not expected to.

By 1965 there were some calls for Daugherty's contract, but the team he turned out that year silenced all complaints, at least until the Rose Bowl. Led by Clint Jones, Charles "Bubba" Smith, and George Webster, it won the national championship with a perfect record. When it got to Pasadena, however, it appeared to let down badly and was outplayed by U.C.L.A. in the surprise of the year. One reason for Daugherty's difficulty in motivating his team was the fact that it had already beaten U.C.L.A. during the regular season.

In the decade of the sixties every Big Ten team except Northwestern won at least one championship. Ohio State and Michigan State were perhaps a bit stronger than the rest, but Minnesota and Michigan each managed to win twice, and Purdue fielded several powerful squads with its traditionally good passing quarterback.

The long line of great throwers continued from West Lafayette, with Bob Griese and Mike Phipps following in the footsteps of Bob DeMoss, Dale Samuels, and Len Dawson.

Minnesota, under one of General Neyland's former players, Murray Warmath, produced a succession of premier defensive linemen, including Bob Bell, Carl Eller, and Aaron Brown. The Gophers had begun the decade with their best team since Bierman's 1941 national champions, but a defeat by Washington in the Rose Bowl brought a gloomy end to the season. Warmath took them back the next year, however, and with Sandy Stephens directing the offense, the Gophers won easily over U.C.L.A.

The Big Ten, which had seen its representatives win twelve of the first thirteen Rose Bowl games from the Pacific Coast Conference's nominees, now had to accustom itself to losing as often as it won at Pasadena. The West, after much travail, had at last begun to recapture some of its lost glory.

Charles "Bubba" Smith, 6'7", 295-pound defensive end at Michigan State in 1965–66. If this Spartan had been at Thermopylae, the Persians would have turned around and gone home.

29. The West Comes Back

At Berkeley in the first years after the war Lynn Waldorf coached three consecutive undefeated teams, two of them untied as well, and sent them into the Rose Bowl with high hopes. But each time they were beaten in the last quarter by their Big Ten adversaries. These California elevens, with Rod Franz and Les Richter in the line and Jackie Jensen in the backfield, were the closest thing to a West Coast dynasty since the Southern California teams coached by Howard Harding Jones in the early thirties. Still, they lacked whatever seemingly magical ingredient it took to defeat the Big Ten representative at Pasadena. It was not until the Southern California champions of 1952 that the West Coast reasserted itself on New Year's Day.

There is a remarkable historical parallel between the accomplishments of the 1952 Trojans and their counterparts of 1969. In 1952 Southern Cal met U.C.L.A., both teams unbeaten, for the Pacific title and Rose Bowl invitation. The Trojans trailed 12–7 in the fourth quarter, but came back to win 14–12. In 1969 Southern Cal met U.C.L.A., both teams unbeaten, for the Pacific title and Rose Bowl invitation. The Trojans again trailed 12–7 in the fourth quarter and again came back to win 14–12.

In the Rose Bowl game that ended the 1952 season Southern Cal faced a twice-defeated Big Ten co-champion (Wisconsin) and won by 7 points on a pass from the quarterback (Bukich) to the wingback (Carmichael). In the Rose Bowl that concluded the 1969 season the Trojans again faced a twice-defeated Big Ten co-champion (Michigan) and again won by 7 points on a pass from the quarterback (Jones) to the wingback (Chandler).

In both 1952 and 1969, moreover, Southern Cal saw its perfect season spoiled at South Bend. A week after winning over U.C.L.A. in 1952, the Trojans were stopped by Notre Dame. And midway through the 1969 season they were tied by the Irish.

The Big Ten teams bounced back from the Wisconsin defeat at Pasadena in 1952 and won six more Rose Bowl games in a row, but the scores this time were closer.

The two meetings between U.C.L.A. and Michigan State were tense, hard-fought affairs in which the Bruins distinguished themselves even in a losing cause. Football at Westwood had made a dramatic upsurge with the coming of Henry Russell "Red" Sanders from Vanderbilt in 1949. U.C.L.A. became known for a powerful and deceptive single wing attack as well as for a sturdy defense. Sanders had been influenced by the philosophy of General Neyland, against whose Tennessee elevens he had both played and coached.

In the four campaigns from 1952 through 1955, the Bruins lost only three regular-season games, one by a single point, one by 2 points, and one by a touchdown. The two Rose Bowl losses to the Spartans were by 8 and 3 points respectively, the latter coming on Dave Kaiser's 41-yard field goal in the last seven seconds.

In 1954, when U.C.L.A. had the greatest team in its history, it was prevented from playing at Pasadena by a Pacific Coast Conference rule, later abolished, barring repeat appearances. The 1954 Bruins were one of the best teams ever developed in the West. They scored 367 points in nine games while allowing only 40. Stanford was humiliated by an unbelievable 72–0, Oregon State by 61–0, and even Southern Cal was mercilessly destroyed 34–0. Only Washington and Maryland gave U.C.L.A. any real difficulty. Jim Tatum's Terrapins bowed by a 12–7 score, but the next year, on a wet field at College Park, they handed U.C.L.A. its lone defeat.

These were the years in which Maryland's split T offense, under the direction of quarterbacks Jack Scarbath and Bernie

Faloney, brought the school three perfect records in five years. But Tatum's luck in postseason games was little better than Sanders'. Maryland lost twice in the Orange Bowl to Oklahoma teams coached by Bud Wilkinson, who had learned the split T with Tatum at the feet of its guru, Don Faurot. Only in the Sugar Bowl game of 1952 did Maryland reach its full capability. There it crushed Tennessee's number-one-ranked Volunteers in a flawless exhibition of offensive and defensive might that left even General Neyland awestruck.

Despite the fact that the Sanders-coached U.C.L.A. teams came to grief at Pasadena, they elevated the sagging prestige of West Coast football.

But it was not until the Washington elevens of 1959 and 1960 that the Coast really showed consistent strength in the Rose Bowl. The Huskies were quarterbacked by a one-eyed daredevil named Bob Schloredt, and when he was on the loose running the split T option play or throwing the ball, Big Ten opponents were badly discomfited. The Huskies had known great backfield performers before, such as Don Heinrich and Hugh McElhenny, but Schloredt had a stronger supporting cast. He and his teammates defeated Wisconsin 44–8 in the most one-sided West Coast victory over the Big Ten. The next year they upset Minnesota's national champions and justifiably claimed the honor for themselves.

During the sixties the Pacific Coast won five and lost five at Pasadena, a profound improvement over its showing in earlier years. No victory was more thrilling than Southern California's 42–37 triumph over Wisconsin in 1963. The game matched the two best teams in the country. The Trojans, striking with speed and power, appeared on the verge of a massacre and led 42–14 as the last quarter began. But Wisconsin came back with the greatest rally in Rose Bowl history to score 23 points. Time, however, ran out on the Badgers and their heroic passing combination of Ron VanderKellen and Pat Richter.

The victory was satisfying to the Coast, but nothing could quite match the jubilation it felt when U.C.L.A. upset

Michigan State's national champions 14–12 in the 1966 game. The Bruins had lost an early-season encounter to the defensively awesome Spartans and had learned from the experience. At Pasadena they played a daring, clever game, forcing the overconfident Big Ten team to make costly mistakes.

U.C.L.A.'s return to eminence in the mid-sixties was tied to the all-round excellence of its Heisman Trophy-winning quarterback, Gary Beban. But if the Bruins were good, Southern California was usually a bit better.

The Trojans were experimenting with a new formation conjured up by coach John McKay. He deployed his backfield in a line perpendicular to the defense and called it the I formation. There were virtually unlimited opportunities for tricky shifts out of the basic alignment. Another feature was the hiding from view of the eventual ballcarrier for a second or two. Often this was enough to confound the linebackers and produce a major gain. It was especially effective when a fast halfback had such extra time, and McKay came up with just the man to make the best use of it.

He was Orenthal James Simpson, one of the great running backs in the history of football—and quite possibly the best of them all. He could run a hundred yards in 9.4 seconds. At 6'1" and 207 pounds, Simpson combined a sprinter's speed with a fullback's power. But speed and drive were not his only assets. He had an astonishing array of movements in the open field which made him extremely difficult to tackle. Playing only two varsity seasons—and against many of the best teams in the nation—Simpson gained a total of 3,124 yards. In 1968 he ran for 1,709 and won the Heisman Trophy.

A year before, in the big game with Beban's U.C.L.A., Southern Cal trailed in the closing minutes when Simpson barged through the Bruin line and raced 64 yards to the winning touchdown. It put the Trojans in the Rose Bowl, gave them the Pacific Coast title, and wrapped up the national championship all in one glorious dash.

Under the intelligent guidance of McKay and the ener-

getic recruiting of his assistants, Southern California flourished in the sixties. It won every game and the national championship in 1962, captured another national title in 1967, and went undefeated in regular-season play in both 1968 and 1969. Ohio State took the national championship away at Pasadena in 1968, but a year later the Trojans handed Michigan its first Rose Bowl defeat. McKay had thus become the most successful Southern Cal coach since Howard Harding Jones, and even the Head Man never took four consecutive teams to Pasadena.

O. J. Simpson of Southern California makes his titanic touchdown dash in the 1967 U.C.L.A. game to win the conference title, national championship, and Rose Bowl bid all on one play.

30. The Dead Kings

"East were the dead kings and the remembered sepulchres," wrote the poet and onetime Yale football player Archibald MacLeish. But if the monarchs of the old Establishment had passed on, their descendants were still very much alive. In the section where the game was born there were more than a few heroes to awaken memories of bygone football glories.

One of the most celebrated was Dick Kazmaier, Princeton's greatest player and the main reason for the Tigers' perfect records in 1950 and 1951. As a triple-threat tailback in coach Charlie Caldwell's single wing offense, Kazmaier excelled in throwing the option pass. He would run wide as if to circle the opposing end. When the defense converged, he calmly lofted the ball far down the field to a waiting receiver. There was not much use in dropping back to cover the targets, however, since Kazmaier would then merely exercise his option and gallop elusively past the defenders.

Caldwell won 70 games and lost 30 in a dozen years, and was especially good at beating Harvard and Yale. He designed his offense around Kazmaier's skills, which were never more in evidence than in the big game of 1951 against powerful Cornell. Both teams were unbeaten, but Kazmaier worked the option play to such perfection that the Big Red was first reduced to frustration and then to despair. The Tigers won a landslide 53–15 victory and swept onward to a perfect season. Kazmaier gained a total of 1,827 yards

Princeton's Dick Kazmaier. The old-timers could have their Cowans, Poes, Whites, and Treats. This was the greatest Tiger of them all.

running and passing to lead the nation, and win the Heisman Trophy easy.

As good as Princeton was, however, it could not overtake such titans as Michigan State, Tennessee, and Oklahoma in the wire-service ratings. It seemed for a long time that no Eastern team ever again would stand at the top of the polls. But in 1959 the Saltine Warriors of Syracuse came up with a mighty aggregation that forced its way to the pinnacle of the lists. It won not only the national championship but also led in scoring, offensive yardage, and defense—the first time that any school had exercised such complete statistical domination. The Orangemen, under veteran coach Ben Schwartzwalder, rolled up 390 points to 59 for ten opponents. Only Penn State and Kansas gave them more than a light scrimmage. The season was then completed in the Cotton Bowl with a 23–14 victory over Southwest Conference champion Texas.

Syracuse displayed an awesome running game—with Ger Schwedes, Ernie Davis, and Art Baker doing the ball carrying —and by far the best line in the country. The school had known great players in previous years, such as Vic Hanson in the twenties and Jim Brown in the mid-fifties, but never had it seen so many on one varsity.

Ernie Davis completed his brilliant career two years later by winning the Heisman Trophy, but tragedy struck soon afterward. While preparing for the College All-Star Game against the professional champions the following summer, he fainted and was rushed to a Chicago hospital. There his ailment was diagnosed as leukemia, and ten months later he was dead.

Davis and two renowned Navy players, Joe Bellino and Roger Staubach, gave the East more than adequate representation on the Heisman Trophy list. Staubach was a clever runner and an accurate passer. He quarterbacked Navy to one of its best seasons in 1963, when it won all but one game. A visit to the Cotton Bowl, however, resulted in a trouncing by the finest Texas team in a generation.

But if the section was falling behind at turning out national champions, at least it could take pride in its individual

Ernie Davis of Syracuse gallops through Kansas at Lawrence in 1960. This was a triumph; the tragedy came later.

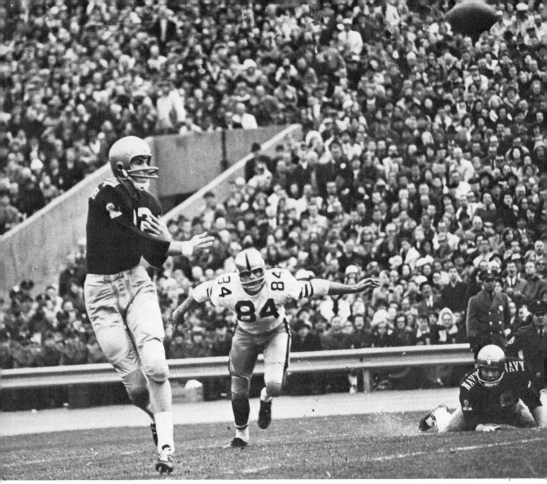

Roger Staubach of Navy, the 1963 Heisman Trophy winner, throws the option pass while running at full speed. He makes it look easy, but it isn't.

stars. It had become difficult, though, for outstanding Ivy League players to gain recognition. This was in spite of the fact that two Yale men, Larry Kelley and Clint Frank, had been among the first three Heisman Trophy winners in the mid-thirties.

Kelley, at end, was an all-around wizard who conjured up at least one miracle in every game. Moreover, he was celebrated for his quick wit and flair for showmanship, qualities which made it certain that when 70,000 fans came to the Yale Bowl, everybody there saw Kelley. Only one other end, Leon Hart of Notre Dame in 1949, has won the Heisman Trophy.

258

Jim Brown of Syracuse carries a couple of T.C.U. defenders along with him in the 1957 Cotton Bowl game. Brown scored all 27 of the Orangemen's points, but T.C.U. made 28.

Frank, who won the award in 1937, was outstanding in every phase of the game. He was as close to being a one-man team as anyone who has ever played. Some measure of Frank's ability may be gained from the fact that he won the trophy over so great a star as Byron White of Colorado.

White was the nation's best in total offense, rushing, and scoring, while leading the Buffaloes to a perfect season. In addition, he won Phi Beta Kappa honors, was class valedictorian, went to Oxford as a Rhodes scholar, and later finished first in his law school class at Yale after having played professional football. He was elevated to the United States Supreme Court in 1962 by President John F. Kennedy. For combined academic and athletic excellence, few men can equal the accomplishments of Justice White. He is one of football's Renaissance men.

Paul Robeson is another. Twice an All-America end at Rutgers, Robeson earned a Phi Beta Kappa key and went on to Columbia Law School. Later he attained world renown both in the opera and on the dramatic stage. Harvard's Barry Wood is another: All-America quarterback, distinguished bacteriologist, and Vice-President of Johns Hopkins. And Jerome "Brud" Holland, All-America end at Cornell, sociologist, college president, and Ambassador to Sweden, is still another.

Easterners insisted, perhaps with exaggerated pride, that such Renaissance men appeared more often on their varsities than on those of any other section. The claim, however, could not be verified but, if true, there were some who felt that it would offer more than adequate compensation for the vanishing of national champions.*

---

* The national champions played elsewhere, but even the Ivy League could produce an unforgettable game occasionally. In 1968, for example, Harvard trailed Yale 29–13 with less than a minute left to play in a game that matched perfect-record teams. With a reserve quarterback named Frank Champi throwing passes all over the field, the Crimson scored, made a 2-point conversion, then recovered an onside kick, scored again, and—unbelievably—made another 2-point conversion to achieve a 29–29 tie. The pass for the tying points was completed in near darkness, and the crowd in Harvard Stadium reacted with the kind of hysterical joy that might have seemed more appropriate in less sophisticated places such as Lincoln or Tuscaloosa.

31. Make Way for the Wishbone

In the world of college football all roads lead to South Bend. They have since that afternoon in 1913 on the plains at West Point when Dorais and Rockne catapulted Notre Dame to the summit of the game. Accordingly, when a new coach is installed under the Golden Dome, it is an event of paramount importance.

Thus an avalanche of publicity descended upon the former Irish halfback Terry Brennan when he succeeded Frank Leahy in 1954, but soon the pressures of the job more than equaled its prestige.

Brennan, himself only a few years older than the seniors on the varsity, had coached Mt. Carmel High School to the Chicago city championship while earning a law degree at DePaul.

His first season at Notre Dame was a rousing success, as Ralph Guglielmi quarterbacked the team to nine victories. Only Purdue, with Len Dawson passing expertly, marred the record. But Brennan had the misfortune to become coach at a time when Notre Dame's seemingly inexhaustible reservoir of talent was beginning to run dry. What made this even more disheartening was the simultaneous upsurge in the manpower of a number of schools on the Irish schedule.

Only the beginnings of the recession showed in 1955, however, as Notre Dame won eight out of ten. But the decline hit bottom with a sickening thud in 1956, when—despite the efforts of Heisman Trophy winner Paul Hornung—Iowa scored 48 points, Michigan State 47, and Oklahoma's

Terry Brennan, coach of Notre Dame in the mid-fifties. He celebrated one Christmas by losing his situation.

national champions 40. Notre Dame lost eight games, its worst season up to that time, and the shock of the alumni gradually gave way to resentment.

Brennan rallied his forces the following year, however, for a monumental upset of Oklahoma, which ended football's longest winning streak. But the Irish were beaten soundly by Michigan State, Iowa, and Navy. After four losses during the next season, Brennan was cast adrift by the school's administration, which cited a "commitment to excellence" as its justification. With astonishing insensitivity, the decision was announced just before Christmas. It provoked a spate of outraged replies from Brennan's many admirers, who felt that a five-year record of 32 victories and 18 defeats warranted better treatment.

But the decision stood, and Joe Kuharich, a former Irish lineman in the mid-thirties, was brought in from the Washington Redskins. The team, however, did not respond to Kuharich's ministrations, losing five games in his first season. This was followed by another debacle in which eight defeats were suffered, including a horrendous 51–19 drubbing by Purdue.

After three more disappointing seasons it became apparent that something less than a commitment to excellence was taking place. Critics called it an acceptance of mediocrity, and the proud Notre Dame victory tradition seemed in danger of eclipse.

Kuharich came in for much blame, as a losing coach always does, but his defenders could argue in return that the caliber of material was still below the school's usual standard. Alumni were mobilized by the unaccustomed adversity, and gradually the cycle reversed itself and a regiment of prize linemen and backs turned up. It came too late to help Kuharich, however. He was replaced in 1964 by Ara Parseghian, the Northwestern coach who had made a specialty of beating Notre Dame.

Parseghian was another of the bright young graduates of Miami University in Oxford, Ohio. In his first season he brought the Irish to the brink of a national championship, only to be thwarted by an inspired Southern California team in the upset of the year.

Notre Dame had won its first nine games to the surprise of nearly all observers. Parseghian had made excellent use of quarterback John Huarte, who was to win the Heisman Trophy, and end Jack Snow. Together they formed the season's most successful passing combination. They were assisted by a host of eager sophomores who had been infused with intense competitive spirit by the dedicated and articulate Parseghian.

It appeared that the first perfect season in fifteen years was at hand when the Irish moved methodically to a 17–0 half-time advantage over Southern Cal. But the Trojans came storming back in the final thirty minutes on the strength of future Heisman Trophy winner Mike Garrett's running and Rod Sherman's miraculous pass receptions. With only a minute and a half remaining, Sherman eluded the Irish secondary and caught the winning touchdown pass. Old Southern Cal fans rejoiced in the memory of a similar triumph thirty-three years before at South Bend.

It was a bitter letdown for the Irish, but the season had nonetheless been a productive one. Notre Dame was now firmly back on the winning track, and Parseghian began building his great 1966 team even in the ashes of defeat.

As seniors, the sophomores of 1964 were augmented by a rookie passing duo which was even better than Huarte and Snow. Terry Hanratty and Jim Seymour began their varsity careers in record-breaking style as the Irish defeated a good Purdue team in the opening game. Seymour caught thirteen of Hanratty's passes, and they kept this up throughout the season as Notre Dame scored 362 points. The aerial game was perfectly balanced by Nick Eddy's brilliant running. And the defense was, if anything, even more spectacular. Anchored by Alan Page, Jim Lynch, and Kevin Hardy, it allowed only 38 points in ten games.

Many Notre Dame men thought that this was the best team in the school's history, and a few were convinced that it was the strongest of all time. Yet it too was denied a perfect season. The stumbling block was Duffy Daugherty's similarly unbeaten and untied Michigan State team, the perennial spoiler of Irish dreams of glory. The Spartans could match Notre Dame man for man at almost every position. On offense they had Clint Jones, Gene Washington, and Bob Apisa,

Winning may not be everything, but it sure is fun. Notre Dame coach Ara Parseghian leaves the 1971 Cotton Bowl after his Irish had just ended Texas's winning streak at thirty games.

and on defense there were George Webster, Al Brenner, and Bubba Smith.

The confrontation came late in November at East Lansing, and the frenzy it generated was reminiscent of the Army–Notre Dame game of 1946. The Irish lost Eddy (who twisted his knee) before the action began, and Hanratty soon after, yet managed to hold the Big Ten champions to a 10–7 half-time margin. State played without Apisa, its star fullback, who had been injured in an earlier game. The second half saw a desperate defensive struggle in which the only points registered were Notre Dame's tying field goal. With scarcely more than a minute remaining and the Irish on their own 30-yard line, quarterback Coley O'Brien, who had passed well in Hanratty's absence, was instructed to run out the clock. Parseghian was content to accept a tie, but the partisan Michigan State crowd booed lustily, and the Spartan defenders taunted Notre Dame players with cries of "Tie one for the Gipper!"

In the week that followed, Michigan State made a strong claim to the national championship, but Parseghian still had one card left to play. Notre Dame, unlike the Spartans, had not completed its schedule. Parseghian thus placed his hopes on a big victory over Southern California. He had two powerful motivational aids: the memory which his seniors had of their defeat at Los Angeles two years before and the rising anger of the whole squad at the implication that it was guilty of a "no win" attitude. The result was a 51–0 massacre of the Trojans, their worst defeat ever. Notre Dame was quickly returned to the top of both wire-service polls and South Bend toasted its first national champion since Leahy's days.

O. J. Simpson brought the title to resurgent Southern Cal the following year, and Ohio State earned it in 1968 with a great team that ran up 50 points against Michigan and beat the Trojans in the Rose Bowl.

The Buckeyes seemed certain to win it again in 1969, with the highest-scoring eleven in modern Big Ten history. Some experts were even saying that Woody Hayes had the greatest team of all time. But at Ann Arbor it encountered a vengeful pack of Wolverines, brilliantly coached by Hayes's

Reggie Cavander of Michigan State runs through the Notre Dame line at East Lansing in 1966. It ended 10–10, and then the arguments began.

Darrell Royal of Texas makes a wish on his new wishbone T formation. Thirty straight wins for the Longhorns was the result.

former chief assistant, Bo Schembechler. Michigan reached the inspirational summit and won one of the classic upset victories by a score of 24–12.

With the Buckeyes out of the running, the national championship thus went to Darrell Royal's finest Texas team, which came from behind to defeat Arkansas by a point. Royal and Frank Broyles of the Razorbacks had become the dominant coaches in the Southwest. Both were former quarterbacks, Royal at Oklahoma under Bud Wilkinson and Broyles at Georgia Tech under Bobby Dodd.

Penn State vigorously disputed the award of the national title to Texas, and there were some who agreed that the

Nittany Lions deserved the prize. Under coach Joe Paterno the Easterners completed two perfect seasons, each time defeating a strong Big Eight champion in the Orange Bowl. Paterno, like Royal and Broyles, had been a quarterback. He was one of Brown University's most astute signal callers, and after graduating in 1950, followed his coach, Rip Engle, to Penn State.

The Nittany Lions' bid for a third consecutive perfect season failed in 1970 when they lost badly to Colorado. But by and large the strong teams of 1969 were still on top a year later, as both Texas and Ohio State won all of their regular-season games and Nebraska went undefeated in the sturdy Big Eight, although tied by Southern California in a nonconference game. Ohio State avenged its upset loss to Michigan in 1969 by playing flawlessly before a record Columbus crowd and winning 20–9 in a contest between perfect-record teams. But both the Buckeyes and Texas were dealt stunning upset defeats on New Year's Day. Notre Dame stopped the Longhorns in the Cotton Bowl, ending their winning streak at thirty. In order to beat Texas the Irish had to contain the nation's foremost running game. They did this in part because of a novel defense which exactly mirrored the Longhorns' wishbone T formation alignment * on offense. In the Rose Bowl, Stanford came from behind in the last quarter on the strength of an inspired defense and the passing of Heisman Trophy winner Jim Plunkett to ruin Ohio State's perfect season, 27–17. With Nebraska winning in the Orange Bowl over a good L.S.U. team, the Corn-

---

* Royal had perfected the wishbone formation, so called because the fullback is stationed a step ahead of his previous position in the T, thus giving the backfield the configuration of a wishbone. From this set the quarterback may exercise the "triple option"; that is, he may hand the ball to his fullback for a plunge into the line, run around either end, or pitch the ball backward to a trailing halfback. Placing the fullback a step closer to the line causes the defense to respect the possibility of a quick plunge and prevents it from concentrating exclusively on containing the quarterback. The formation had taken hold at many schools as the seventies began. The offense had thus once again confounded the defense but, as in the past, defensive strategists were at work on the antidote. For all its explosiveness, the wishbone had its liabilities. The pitchouts could be fumbled, and most coaches felt that it was a poor formation from which to throw a long pass.

huskers claimed the national championship and the Associated Press poll agreed.

As exciting as the games were in 1970, however, the real story of the season was one of unprecedented tragedy. Two catastrophic airplane crashes blighted the year and made it incomparably the saddest in the entire history of the sport. At midseason thirteen Wichita State University players and their coach died in the crash of one of the team's chartered planes in the Rockies. It seemed as though no greater misfortune could befall any team, and yet only a few weeks later thirty-eight Marshall University players were to die in the worst disaster in the sport's history. Returning from a losing game with East Carolina, the entire Marshall team and its coach perished when its plane crashed on a hillside near the Huntington, West Virginia, airport, almost within sight of the campus. In the stunned and grieving aftermath the university announced that it would continue the game in 1971, and expressions of sympathy and support came to the school from all over the nation. Whatever the future held, however, there would always remain the haunting memory of Marshall's 1970 team, only a modest one by its record, but one which by the whim of the unfathomable gods would play all the rest of its games on the eternal green of the Elysian fields.

32. A Footnote on 1971 and 1972

The past two seasons are so fresh in memory that it is necessary only to list their highlights. It is enough to say that in 1971 Nebraska and Oklahoma were easily the two best teams, that their meeting on Thanksgiving Day at Norman was incontestably the game of the year, and possibly of the decade as well, and that the Cornhuskers' last-minute 35–31 victory was the most exciting moment of the season. With Nebraska winning the national championship, Oklahoma finishing second, and Colorado third, it marked the first time that one conference had captured the top three places in the Associated Press poll. Long forgotten was the time when the disdainful could put down the Big Eight by labeling it nothing more than Oklahoma and the Seven Dwarfs.

In the Rose Bowl, Stanford repaid a debt of seventy years' standing when it upset Michigan 13–12 on a last-second field goal, thereby spoiling the Wolverines' first perfect season in a generation. Stanford thus avenged its 49–0 humiliation at Michigan's hands in the first Rose Bowl game.

Led by its sensational sophomore halfback Anthony Davis, Southern California dominated the 1972 season, winning every game, including an awesome 42–17 Rose Bowl victory over Ohio State, on the strength of a balanced offense and an opportunistic defense. Davis reached his zenith by scoring an unprecedented six touchdowns against Notre Dame, two on long kick-off returns, in a performance that evoked memories of Red Grange's one-man show against Michigan in 1924.

On the opening Saturday of the 1971 season, Marshall University kept a promise and sent its newly assembled team out to meet Morehead State. Marshall lost that day by three touchdowns, but a week later it played Xavier and won 15–13.

Epilogue

Whenever football has been criticized, there have always been those who leaped to its defense with the claim that certain moral benefits were conferred upon its participants. All sorts of wondrous qualities—such as sportsmanship, maturity, understanding, and even love of one's fellow man— were said to be inherent in this strange and violent game which so profoundly mingles the elements of chess, geometry, and warfare.

And yet despite the vulnerability of such rationalizations, there may be at least a grain of truth in them. Football is, after all, a social institution of considerable antiquity in a society which deeply, almost pathetically, yearns for some sense of continuity and tradition. Institutions have endured far longer with much less justification.

If the Toynbees of a later time should decide that our ruins indicate that violence was the mortal disease of this age, then football will not have been much of a help.

There are those, however, who agree with that sage of sports commentators, Heywood Hale Broun, that watching the action on the gridiron somehow reduces the desire to pummel one's neighbor. But there are also disturbing emanations from the laboratory of Professor Leonard Berkowitz at the University of Wisconsin to the effect that the witnessing of mayhem increases the desire in Homo sapiens to do likewise.

If, however, the malignancy of this era should turn out to have been bigotry, then perhaps such seemingly frivolous games as football may have a deeper relevance. It is manifest that an athletic team will only reflect the tensions of the society of which it is a part, and it would be too much to expect that it should somehow be able to transcend them. Yet in desperate times, in a nation so terribly riven by ethnic hatreds, perhaps one may hope that at least on rare occasions and for a few precious moments this might be the case. It is a faint hope, but the thought that it may not be altogether in vain is reinforced by the research of a great scholar. "The principle," wrote the renowned Harvard psychologist Gordon W. Allport in his classic *The Nature of Prejudice*, "is clearly illustrated in the multi-ethnic athletic team. Here the goal is all-important; the ethnic composition of the team is irrelevant. It is the cooperative striving for the goal that engenders solidarity."

If Professor Allport is indeed correct, then we may be justified in believing that a touchdown is, and always has been, one of those rare human events devoid of caste, race, or previous condition of servitude. It is merely six points and a good yell (or groan), and as such may it ever be thus.

Formations

T FORMATION
*(balanced line, i.e., three
men on each side of the center)*

**SINGLE WING
FORMATION**
*(unbalanced line, strong side
to the right)*

DOUBLE WING FORMATION
(unbalanced line, strong right)

SPLIT T FORMATION

E - END	Q - QUARTERBACK	SE - SPLIT END
T - TACKLE	H - HALFBACK	TE - TIGHT END
G - GUARD	TB - TAILBACK	FL - FLANKER
C - CENTER	F - FULLBACK	W - WINGBACK

E T G C G T E
Q
F
H   H

WISHBONE T FORMATION

E T G C G T E
Q   W
H   H

WING T FORMATION

E T G C G T E
Q
            H
F
T

I FORMATION

E T G C G T E
Q
            H
F
TB

POWER I FORMATION

SE   T G C G T TE
Q
                FL
F   H

T FORMATION
WITH SPLIT END ON THE LEFT AND
FLANKER BACK ON THE RIGHT

Team Nicknames

Alabama	Crimson Tide
Arkansas	Razorbacks
Army	Cadets; Black Knights
Auburn	Plainsmen; Tigers
Baylor	Bears
Boston College	Eagles
Brown	Bruins
California	Golden Bears
Carlisle	Indians
Carnegie Tech	Engineers; Tartans
Centre	Praying Colonels
Chicago	Maroons
Colgate	Red Raiders
Colorado	Golden Buffaloes
Columbia	Lions
Cornell	the Big Red
Dartmouth	the Big Green; Indians
Duke	Blue Devils
Fordham	Rams
Georgetown	Hoyas
Georgia	Bulldogs
Georgia Tech	Engineers; Yellowjackets
Harvard	the Crimson
Illinois	Fighting Illini
Indiana	Hoosiers
Iowa	Hawkeyes

Kansas	Jayhawks
Kentucky	Wildcats
Louisiana State	Bengal Tigers
Maryland	Terrapins
Michigan	the Maize and Blue; Wolverines
Michigan State	Spartans
Minnesota	Golden Gophers
Mississippi	Rebels
Missouri	Tigers
Navy	Midshipmen
Nebraska	Cornhuskers
North Carolina	Tarheels
Northwestern	the Purple; Wildcats
Notre Dame	Fighting Irish
Ohio State	Buckeyes; the Scarlet and Gray
Oklahoma	Sooners
Oregon	Ducks; Webfoots
Oregon State	Beavers
Penn State	Nittany Lions
Pennsylvania	Quakers; the Red and Blue
Pittsburgh	Panthers
Princeton	Tigers
Purdue	Boilermakers
Rice	Owls
Rutgers	Scarlet Knights
Southern California	Trojans
Southern Methodist	Mustangs
Stanford	Cardinals; Indians (nickname dropped in 1972)
Syracuse	Orangemen; Saltine Warriors
Tennessee	Volunteers
Texas	Longhorns
Texas A. & M.	Aggies
Texas Christian	Horned Frogs
Tulane	Green Wave
U.C.L.A.	Bruins; Uclans
Vanderbilt	Commodores
Washington	Huskies
Washington & Jefferson	Presidents
Washington State	Cougars
Wisconsin	Badgers
Yale	the Blue; Bulldogs; Elis

Bibliography

Allport, Gordon W. *The Nature of Prejudice.* Reading: Addison-Wesley Publishing Co., 1954.

Baker, Louis Henry. *Football: Facts and Figures.* New York: Rinehart and Co., 1945.

Beach, James C., and David Moore. *Army vs. Notre Dame: The Big Game, 1913–1947.* New York: Random House, 1948.

Bealle, Morris, A. *Gangway for Navy.* Washington, D.C.: Columbia Publishing Co., 1951.

————. *The History of Football at Harvard, 1874–1948.* Washington, D.C.: Columbia Publishing Co., 1948.

Bishop, Morris. *A History of Cornell.* Ithaca: Cornell University Press, 1962.

Blaik, Earl Henry, with Tim Cohane. *You Have to Pay the Price.* New York: Holt, Rinehart and Winston, 1960.

Boda, Steve. *College Football All-Time Record Book, 1869–1969.* New York: National Collegiate Athletic Association, 1969.

Brown, Warren. *Rockne.* Chicago: Reilly and Lee Co., 1931.

Buchanan, Lamont. *The Story of Football in Text and Pictures.* New York: Vanguard Press, 1951.

Camp, Walter Chauncey. *American Football.* New York: Harper & Brothers, 1894.

Carlson, Stanley W. *Dr. Henry L. Williams: A Football Biography.* Minneapolis: S. W. Carlson, 1938.

Claassen, Harold. *Football's Unforgettable Games.* New York: Ronald Press, 1963.

————, with Steve Boda. *Ronald Encyclopedia of Football.* New York: Ronald Press, 1960.

Cohane, Timothy. *Bypaths of Glory.* New York: Harper & Row, 1963.

————. *Gridiron Grenadiers.* New York: G. P. Putnam's Sons, 1948.

Crisler, Herbert Orin. *Modern Football: Fundamentals and Strategy*. New York: Whittlesey House, 1949.

Danzig, Allison. *The History of American Football*. Englewood Cliffs: Prentice-Hall, 1956.

Davis, Parke Hill. *Football: The American Intercollegiate Game*. New York: Charles Scribner's Sons, 1911.

Edson, James S. *Alabama's Crimson Tide*. Montgomery: The Paragon Press, 1947.

Fitzgerald, Edward, ed. *Kick-off!* New York: Bantam Books, 1948.

Grange, Harold Edward. *Zuppke of Illinois*. New Haven: Glaser, 1937.

Grothe, Peter, ed. *Great Moments in Stanford Sports*. Palo Alto: Pacific Books, 1952.

Harris, Reed. *King Football*. New York: Vanguard Press, 1932.

Heffelfinger, W. W. *This Was Football*. New York: Barnes, 1954.

Herring, Donald Grant. *Forty Years of Football*. New York: Carlyle House, 1940.

Hill, Dean. *Football Thru the Years*. New York: Gridiron Publishing Co., 1940.

Hollander, Zander, ed. *Strange But True Football Stories*. New York: Random House, 1967.

Koger, Jim. *Football's Greatest Games*. Montgomery: Morros Publishing Co., 1966.

Kramer, Jerry, and Dick Schaap. *Instant Replay: The Green Bay Diary of Jerry Kramer*. New York: Norton, 1968.

Lamb, Dick, and B. McGrane. *Seventy-five Years with the Fighting Hawkeyes*. Dubuque: William C. Brown Co., 1964.

Leahy, Frank William. *Notre Dame Football*. Englewood Cliffs: Prentice-Hall, 1949.

Leckie, Robert. *The Story of Football*. New York: Random House, 1965.

Levy, Bill. *Three Yards and a Cloud of Dust*. Cleveland: World Publishing Co., 1966.

Lombardi, Vince, and W. C. Heinz. *Run to Daylight*. Englewood Cliffs: Prentice-Hall, 1963.

Miller, Richard I. *The Truth About Big-Time Football*. New York: Sloane, 1953.

Morison, Samuel E. *Three Centuries of Harvard, 1636–1936*. Boston: Harvard University Press, 1936.

Morse, Clinton. *California Football History*. Berkeley: The Gillick Press, 1937.

Nemerov, Howard. *The Homecoming Game*. New York: Simon and Schuster, 1957.

Newcombe, Jack. *The Fireside Book of Football*. New York: Simon and Schuster, 1964.

Peterson, James Andrew. *Eckersall of Chicago*. Chicago: Hinckley and Schmitt, 1957.

Plimpton, George. *Paper Lion*. New York: Harper & Row, 1966.

Pope, Edwin. *Football's Greatest Coaches*. Atlanta: Tupper and Love, 1956.

Ratcliff, Harold V. *The Power and the Glory*. Lubbock: Texas Tech Press, 1957.

Rice, Grantland. *The Tumult and the Shouting*. Cranbury: A. S. Barnes, 1962.

Roberts, Howard. *The Big Nine*. New York: G. P. Putnam's Sons, 1948.

Russell, Fred, and George Leonard. *Big Bowl Football*. New York: Ronald Press, 1963.

Sagendorph, Kent. *Michigan: The Story of the University*. New York: E. P. Dutton, 1948.

Samuelson, Rube C. *The Rose Bowl Game*. New York: Doubleday and Co., 1951.

Schmidt, George P. *Princeton and Rutgers: The Two Colonial Colleges of New Jersey*. New Brunswick: Rutgers University Press, 1964.

Shaughnessy, Clark Daniel. *Football in War & Peace*. Clinton: Jacobs Press, 1943.

Siler, Thomas T. *The Volunteers*. Knoxville: Knoxville News-Sentinel Publishing Co., 1950.

Stegeman, John F. *Ghosts of Herty Field: Early Days on a Southern Gridiron*. Athens: University of Georgia Press, 1966.

Tips, Kern. *Football, Texas Style*. New York: Doubleday and Co., 1964.

Wallace, Francis. *Dementia Pigskin*. New York: Rinehart and Co., 1951.

———. *Notre Dame: From Rockne to Parseghian*. New York: David McKay Co., rev. ed., 1967.

Walsh, Christy. *College Football and All-America Review*. Hollywood: House-Warven, 1951.

Ward, Archie. *Frank Leahy and the Fighting Irish*. New York: G. P. Putnam's Sons, 1964.

Weyand, Alexander M. *Football Immortals*. New York: The Macmillan Co., 1962.

———. *The Saga of American Football*. New York: The Macmillan Co., 1955.

Index

284

287